111
BUSINESSES YOU CAN START FOR UNDER $10,000

Bantam Business Books

Ask your bookseller for the titles you have missed

CASHING IN ON THE AMERICAN DREAM by Paul Terhorst
COMPLETE GUIDE TO OWNING A HOME-BASED BUSINESS by
the Editors of *Entrepreneur*
DOING IT NOW by Edwin Bliss
EFFECTIVE LISTENING by Kevin J. Murphy
GET TO THE POINT by Karen Berg & Andrew Gilman with
Edward P. Stevenson
GETTING THINGS DONE by Edwin Bliss
GUERRILLA TACTICS IN THE JOB MARKET by Tom Jackson
HOW TO BUY STOCKS by Louis Engel & Brendan Boyd
IACOCCA by Lee Iacocca & William Novak
LEADER EFFECTIVENESS TRAINING by Thomas Gordon
MARKETING YOURSELF by Catalyst Group Staff
MCDONALD'S: BEHIND THE ARCHES by John F. Love
MOLLOY'S LIVE FOR SUCCESS by John T. Molloy
NO BULL SELLING by Hank Trisler
NO NONSENSE MANAGEMENT by Richard S. Sloma
184 BUSINESSES ANYONE CAN START AND MAKE A LOT OF
MONEY, 2nd Edition by the Editors of *Entrepreneur*
168 MORE BUSINESSES ANYONE CAN START AND MAKE A LOT
OF MONEY, 2nd Edition by the Editors of *Entrepreneur*

THE ONLY INVESTMENT GUIDE YOU'LL EVER NEED by Andrew
Tobias
THE ONLY OTHER INVESTMENT GUIDE YOU'LL EVER NEED by
Andrew Tobias
PAY YOURSELF WHAT YOU'RE WORTH by Shirley Hutton with
Constance deSwaan
PERFECT SALES PRESENTATION by Robert L. Shook
THE RENEWAL FACTOR by Robert H. Waterman, Jr.
ROBERT HALF WAY TO GET HIRED IN TODAY'S JOB MARKET by
Robert Half
TALKING STRAIGHT by Lee Iacocca & Sonny Kleinfield
THE TAO OF LEADERSHIP by John Heider
220 BEST FRANCHISES TO BUY by Constance Jones & The Philip
Lief Group
WHAT THEY DON'T TEACH YOU AT HARVARD BUSINESS
SCHOOL by Mark H. McCormack
WHAT THEY *STILL* DON'T TEACH YOU AT HARVARD BUSINESS
SCHOOL by Mark H. McCormack
THE WINNING PERFORMANCE by Donald K. Clifford, Jr. &
Richard C. Cavanaugh
YOU CAN NEGOTIATE ANYTHING by Herb Cohen

Entrepreneur.

MAGAZINE'S

111

BUSINESSES YOU CAN
START FOR UNDER
$10,000

THE EDITORS OF
Entrepreneur.

BANTAM BOOKS
NEW YORK · TORONTO · LONDON · SYDNEY · AUCKLAND

111 BUSINESSES YOU CAN START FOR UNDER $10,000
A Bantam Book / April 1991

Library of Congress Cataloging-in-Publication Data

111 businesses you can start for under $10,000 / the editors of
Entrepreneur.
    p.   cm.
ISBN 0-553-35237-7
  1. New business enterprises.   2. Small business.   3. Success in
business.   1. Entrepreneur (Santa Monica, Calif.)   II. Title: One
hundred eleven businesses you can start for under $10,000.
HD62.5.A135   1991
658.1'141—dc20   90-38245
                                                                      CIP

Published simultaneously in the United States and Canada

PRINTED IN THE UNITED STATES OF AMERICA

OPM   0 9 8 7 6 5 4 3 2 1

INTRODUCTION

The 1990s—there has never been a better time to start and operate your own business. Even the United States Congress recognizes the entrepreneurial revolution currently underway in America and has declared the 1990s to be "The Decade of the Entrepreneur."

Every year, over one million Americans join this entrepreneurial revolution. In fact, business ownership has become one of the nation's biggest status symbols. Why? Some say they're fed up working hard to put money in someone else's pocket. Many believe they're underpaid and unappreciated for what they do. Others seek the satisfaction that only "charting your own course" brings. Whatever the reason, these entrepreneurial "recruits" have signed into an army over twenty million strong and growing.

Wouldn't you like to be one of them? Well, you can be. It's not as difficult or as frightening as you may think. At *Entrepreneur*® magazine, we know that business ownership serves as a great equalizer. There is no discrimination against a great new product or a much needed service. There are no "glass ceilings" to bump your head against. It doesn't matter what race, religion, or sex you are. Age is of no importance. Over the seventeen years we've been in business, we've seen successful businesses started by sixteen-year-olds, as well as those over sixty.

You're probably wondering, if entrepreneurship is so great, why aren't there more entrepreneurs? What keeps so many from business ownership? Fear! People are afraid they don't have enough money to start a business. Or they can't think of a good business idea. Or they mistakenly think that their job offers them security, while entrepreneurship is too risky.

But taking the risk is essential to receiving the rewards. Remember (at the risk of sounding like a high school coach), if you don't swing the bat, you'll never get a hit.

We're not saying that starting your own business is easy. It's not! But almost every entrepreneur we've ever met says the hard work that business start-up entails is worth it. Nothing, they say, equals the satisfaction and rewards (both financially and psychologically) of business ownership.

And, believe it or not, you don't need a lot of money to get started. Many of today's most successful entrepreneurs started their now-giant corporations out of their homes (or garages) on a very limited budget.

What about the idea? That's probably the easiest part. You don't necessarily have to reinvent the wheel. There are thousands of great ideas out there waiting for you to run with them. You don't have to be the first at anything to succeed. McDonalds was not the first hamburger joint. And the Colonel certainly did not invent fried chicken.

What you do need to do is be alert. Look around your community. What's lacking? Is someone doing something you could do better? Or quicker? Or cheaper? Chances are if there's a product or service you're personally seeking, but can't find, others in your area want it too. And they'd be willing to pay for it. Question your friends, neighbors, and relatives. Find the common thread.

Simply reading this book may be the spark you've been looking for. It is just one in a series from the editors of *Entrepreneur*® magazine. In it (and the others) you'll find hundreds of ideas for businesses you can start NOW!

Most important, you need to get started. A successful business owner once told me, "The biggest obstacle to business success is the four words, 'I think I'll wait.'" Don't let this happen to you. If you dream of someday owning your own business, pursue it. Sure, you're going to encounter obstacles and setbacks along the way. But determination and persistence pay off. You can turn your dreams into reality. Only one thing can hold you back: not getting started. Remember these words, written by Goethe, an 18th-century poet, "Whatever you can do or dream, begin it. Boldness has genius, power and magic in it. Begin it now!"

Rieva Lesonsky, Editor
Entrepreneur® magazine

CONTENTS

4

MEDIA BLITZ

5

CAREER AND FINANCIAL SERVICES

6

ON THE ROAD

7

GET YOUR PROMOTION

8
THE FIX IS IN

9
THE PERSONAL TOUCH

10
TOP DOGS AND FAT CATS

11
'TIS THE SEASON

12
TAKING CARE

13
FOR GREEN THUMBS ONLY

14
THE TOURIST TRADE

15
BUSINESS TO BUSINESS

16

KIDS, KIDS, KIDS

17

RETAILING

18

DESIGNING BUSINESSES

19
AUTO SERVICES

20
ODDS AND ENDS

111

BUSINESSES YOU CAN START FOR UNDER $10,000

1

GIFTS THAT KEEP ON GIVING

GIFT BASKET SERVICE

Business:

Assembling and selling (either retail or wholesale) decorated baskets of gifts

Basic Equipment and Expenses:

$5,000

Necessities:

A supply of baskets and enough interesting, unique gift items to fill them

Experience Required:

A flair for shopping and packaging; marketing smarts

Inside Tip:

Prepare for success: This is not a sleepy cottage industry. If your business takes off, you'll have enough work to keep you busy 40, 50, 60 hours a week or more.

It happens to the best of us. It's Christmas (or Hanukkah, a wedding, anniversary, baby shower, birthday, or National Sister-In-Law Appreciation Day). You need the perfect gift, but you don't know the right blouse size. Or the person's taste in books. Or their interests, hobbies, likes or dislikes. All you know is that you have to buy a gift and you can't bring yourself to buy another box of candy or prefabricated bouquet of flowers.

Now what? For consumers lucky enough to find a gift basket service, the problem is solved. All across the country, gift basket services are delivering just what the shopper ordered: imaginative gifts with panache. And for the business owners behind these baskets, low start-up costs and steady demand make this a prime opportunity.

Meesh Miller, owner of The Care Basket in Boulder, Colorado, started her business from home in 1984. "I made a basket for a relative who had had an operation," Miller says. "She asked me to make one for her friend who was also out of commission. When she asked, she offered to pay me for doing it, and it was then I thought there were probably other people who would want the same thing." Through word-of-mouth advertising, direct mail, and write-ups in the local and national press, The Care Package truly took off, keeping Miller hopping sixty hours a week. "My little business is bursting at the seams!" she says.

What goes into a gift basket? Just about anything that fits. From gourmet foods and cookware to bath accessories and handmade crafts, any theme is fair game. Many gift basket services don't manufacture their own goods—they merely assemble all the elements into an attractive parcel. To that end, your packaging skills and your imagination must be particularly keen. This is no business for the mediocre gift buyer.

Gift basket services have two primary markets: retail shoppers (mostly women who, like it or not, do most of the family gift shopping) and corporate accounts. Both have potential but, according to many operators we spoke to, corporate accounts are especially lucrative. Corporate clients need gifts for employees and clients alike—for Christmas, birthdays, anniversaries, promotions, get-well wishes, department awards, and so on.

Beth K. Whiting of Phoenix deals with a variety of corporate clients at her gift basket service, The Beary Sweet Company. "I've worked for many large companies in the past, so I know what their needs are," she says. Whiting's distinctive arrangements of teddy bears bearing sweets make ideal client gifts and display pieces for local businesses and corporations. Whiting launched her business in 1986 on an initial investment of just over $1,000. Within five months, she was in the black. Today, her business is busier than ever.

"I help people tell other people how much they care," says Whiting. "That's a lot of fun."

For More Information:

Gift Association of America
1511 K Street N.W., Suite 716
Washington, D.C. 20005
(202) 638-6080

BALLOON DESIGN AND DELIVERY

Business:

Delivering balloon bouquets and gifts to consumers and/or creating balloon sculptures and displays for weddings, grand openings, and special events

Basic Equipment and Expenses:

$2,500

Necessities:

Transportation, telephone, balloons, helium tank, air pump, twine, gifts if your service includes balloon bouquet and gift delivery, portfolio of photos if you plan to do sculptures and designs

Experience Required:

None, although a book or class on balloon sculpture will save you the hassle of trial and error

Inside Tip:

Balloon baron Charles Prosper suggests looking in the classi-fied section of your local paper for class reunion listings. "People are crying out for this service, but they don't see it unless you promote it," Prosper says.

Time was, balloons were little more than hot air. But thanks to the growing gift and special-events industries, balloons have become the center of a hot business opportu-nity. Here is the story of two aspects of balloon business: bouquet delivery and decoration services. Each has the po-tential for both low start-up and high profits, given the right combination of skills, marketing, and management.

Balloons have become the flowers of the nineties. Not long ago, the only bouquets in town consisted of roses and mums. Consumers now have a choice of Mylar or rubber, helium or air. And where flowers used to be the main decoration at parties, weddings, and special events, balloon arches, spi-rals, and sculptures are now the rage. Balloons have more going for them than mere novelty. From a business perspec-tive, they're cheaper than flowers, easier to store, and they aren't perishable.

According to Charles Prosper, owner of Balloons By Prosper in Los Angeles, there's plenty of room for newcomers in this industry. "There's no better time to go into the balloon business than now," he maintains. "It's still in its infancy— especially in certain parts of the country. California seems to be the hotbed of balloon businesses. But the farther away you get from here, the opportunities get better and better and still better."

Prosper got into the business in 1978, selling balloons on street corners. When that venture failed to pay his bills, he expanded into balloon delivery, then into sculptures, arches, and other elaborate projects. The idea was an unqualified hit. "I became overwhelmed by the business I attracted," Prosper says. "I saw there was more business out there than I could handle." Now he's such a believer that he hosts seminars on balloon art nationwide and overseas, and has even written a book on the subject.

The keys to success, Prosper believes, are training and marketing. Once you've learned the basics of balloon sculpture, just about everything else is sales. Prosper got his service up and running by approaching every wedding and party facility in his community and offering managers a 10 percent commission on any balloon orders they brought in. In turn, they gave him lists of bookings for their facilities. Then Prosper contacted these people directly to offer his services as a decorator. With persistent marketing, Prosper eventually built his business into a $200,000 a year operation.

"You can get into this business on a shoestring without getting yourself into trouble," says Prosper. "In fact, you can hold your nine-to-five job while you're starting out by seeing clients in the evenings and doing the decorations on the weekends. When you start making more money part-time than you do forty hours a week, you'll know it's time to quit your job."

NOVELTY SIGN RENTAL

Business:

Renting out novelty signs announcing births, weddings, and other special occasions

Basic Equipment and Expenses:

$5,000

Necessities:

Telephone, transportation, marketing materials; wood, paint, sandpaper, and saws to construct the signs

Experience Required:

Good marketing and communication skills are important

Inside Tip:

Baby announcements are among the most common in this business, but consider other possibilities. Weddings, birthdays, and Mother's Day are just a few occasions that might also warrant a sign.

In August of 1982, Joni Rosendahl gave birth to a bouncing baby boy. This news delighted her friends Robert and Debra Russell so much that they fashioned a wooden sign in the shape of a stork and installed it on Joni's lawn as a standing announcement of the new arrival. The stork's blue bundle told everyone in the Rosendahl's neighborhood that the newest Rosendahl was a boy.

Of course, Joni was thrilled by the gesture, but she didn't appreciate its full significance immediately. After it was on display a week or so, she retired the stork to storage. But a few weeks later, an agitated neighbor knocked on the Rosendahl's door. His wife had just delivered, he said, and could he rent that stork?

Rosendahl and her friends became the proud parents of Rent-a-Stork, a Portland, Oregon-based sign rental business with licensees around the country. As the name implies, Rosendahl rents out her flock of stork announcements on a weekly basis to new parents in her area. Start-up is low in this business—just enough to cover the cost of making the signs. Profits, on the other hand, are high. "Each stork itself is paid for after only three rentals." Joni says. "After that, delivery costs are all you pay for."

Though no particular experience is required in this business, marketing skills are a must. Being able to generate enthusiasm for the concept will help your fledgling business fly. Between local publicity and marketing through hospitals, baby clinics, and baby shops, Rent-a-Stork has snowballed into a booming business. Today, there are over 100 Rent-a-Stork reps.

LETTER-WRITING SERVICE

Business:

Writing, designing, and sending personal letters on behalf of clients

Basic Equipment and Expenses:

$10,000

Necessities:

Telephone, advertising, paper and stationery supplies; computer with desktop publishing software and laser printer essential once a steady volume is established

Experience Required:

Good writing and listening skills required; a flair for packaging and promotion also handy

Inside Tip:

As an auxiliary service, you can offer personal thank-you notes for businesspeople.

The last time you "said it with flowers," did you wonder how eloquent you were being? Flowers are a classic gesture of goodwill, but sometimes the situation calls for a more direct approach. For instance, what if you need an imaginative way to propose marriage? Suppose you need a creative apology to prevent your wife from packing her bags? Where do you turn for a well-written eulogy?

Beverly Hills, California, letter-writer Martine Greber has the answer. Greber's four-year-old firm, Love Letters Ink, composes and designs letters for all occasions. "It's a way for people to make that important emotional connection," says Greber. "Everyone has a box of old letters that they've saved over the years. They can read those letters years later and feel that same feeling over again. That's something you can't say about flowers."

Greber started her letter-writing service in 1986, after accidentally coming across a Yellow-Page ad for love letters. At the time, she was doing public relations work and wanted additional services to list in her own marketing materials. Love letter writing appealed to her instantly. She contacted local florists and merchants: about thirty of them agreed to carry her services.

That arrangement had its problems. "The turnover in their shops was so great that no one there knew anything about my business," Greber explains. "And, of course, they were getting a cut." Greber decided instead to promote the business through ads in local papers and regional magazines—and she's much happier with the results.

Finding the right marketing wasn't the only hitch. At

first, Greber produced the letters in calligraphy by hand. Hand lettering was an ideal way to start out slowly (the investment was basically the cost of a pen). But as volume grew, Greber needed to computerize. Now, her letters are produced on a laser printer in a calligraphy font.

According to Greber, a good letter-writer must be half author, half therapist. "There are times when we all have trouble saying what we want to say," she says. "You have to be good at communication, and especially communication of emotion. I come from a family of psychologists, and that's helped." Writing on another person's behalf is a special skill, Greber says. "The first love letters I wrote were just awful," she says, "It's hard to put yourself in the place of a fifty-five-year-old man, for example. You develop a talent as you go."

The roughly 1,500 letters Greber wrote in 1988 ran the gamut from wedding vows to wedding toasts, eulogies to apologies. Prices start at $12.95 for a prewritten, personalized letter to $34.95 for a custom job. Although her service is "getting busier every day," Greber admits that it's been hard work establishing a market for her services. "I'd like people to think of letters for all occasions," she says. "I want them to think of this just like they think of roses or candy."

In the meantime, Greber has more than enough work to keep her interest up. "We hear about a lot of interesting situations around here," she says. "It's like a soap opera all the time."

NOVELTY TELEGRAMS

Business:

Delivering personal messages with panache

Basic Equipment and Expenses:

$3,000

Necessities:

Telephone, transportation, costumes (rental possible), props, advertising

Experience Required:

Must have talent and be able to spot it; marketing ability a plus; sense of humor essential

Inside Tip:

Scout around your local area for sources of talent. Theater and music schools are a good bet.

In most major cities, people know who to call for a singing telegram. But where do you find a good gorilla when you need one? And what if you've got a 500-pound male stripper in mind? Novelty telegram services are the answer. While traditional singing telegrams are still a staple of the novelty-gram industry, some firms—like Cleveland's Sweet Revenge, Inc.— take their spoofing one step beyond.

Sweet Revenge founder Richard Radey's motto is, "If it's funny, we'll do it." And that includes serving a pig on a leash in place of pork chops and jumping out of an airplane with a happy-birthday banner. While Radey admits that some gags exceed even his zany sensibilities, he also observes that going all out is part of the business. "You have to find a niche," he says. "You have to do something that no one else is doing."

If running a want-ad for a transvestite belly dancer or delivering X-rated balloons is more than you can handle, remember that practical jokes aren't the only avenue open in the novelty telegram business. In our research, we spotted hula-grams, backrub delivery networks, and celebrity impersonator agencies. The only limit, it seems, is your imagination.

Novelty telegrams are a relatively inexpensive business to start. "Since I was penniless at the time I started mine, I guess you could say it's possible to start out with nothing," says Radey. Yet, given the difficulties of starting on a shoestring, he recommends launching your business with as much capital as possible. Some of Radey's essential expenses: unusual costumes, props, and "a good ad in the Yellow Pages."

At an average price of $85 to $95, Radey's Sweet Revenges aren't cheap. His typical client has a special event in mind—for instance a wedding gag or office-party prank. Because his antics are likely to be the main event of any gathering, he stresses the importance of being reliable. "The worst thing that can happen in this business is not showing up," he explains. "You have 200 people waiting for you to be there. If you aren't, they are going to be upset."

Finding help that's talented, versatile, and reliable isn't easy, according to Radey. "It's a tremendous business if you can find the personnel," he says. "There are tons of advantages to starting a business like this, but the biggest disadvantage is having to find reliable people." Currently, Radey employs some fifty part-timers whom he values enormously. "When you do find good people, you try hard to keep them happy," he says. "Before you start, make sure your resources are good. You need a lot of good people to work with if you want to succeed."

LET THEM SEND CAKE

> People send flowers, so why not cakes? Debora Tsakoumakis explains how careful cost cutting and old-fashioned perseverance helped a new concept take root.

Boulder, Colorado, entrepreneur Debora Tsakoumakis is the first to admit that her cake delivery network hasn't put a Mercedes in her driveway. In 1988, HB Bakery Connection grossed about $20,000; this year Tsakoumakis expects to gross twice that. With the high cost of toll-free telephone service, she's sometimes lucky to break even. Her business isn't the new McDonald's—yet. But thanks to careful cost-cutting and old-fashioned persistence, Tsakoumakis has developed a successful concept that's entirely her own.

Tsakoumakis started her home-based business with a desk, a typewriter, a two-line phone, business stationery, and a supply of red-and-white promotional posters. Altogether, it cost her $1,000. Tsakoumakis admits she's invested more time than money into the business—and at times her small budget has slowed progress. On the other hand, low overhead has kept her from folding: "Last summer I hit a slump," she says. "If I'd had to pay rent, it would have been tough going."

Despite the financial constraints, Tsakoumakis is sure her concept is a winner. HB Bakery Connection allows customers to send cakes to friends, relatives, and business associates in cities around the country—just as they would flowers. Customers place their orders with Tsakoumakis, then she calls on one of the nearly 600 local bakeries in her network to deliver the goods.

Tsakoumakis got the idea for her company in January of 1987. "It was my Dad's birthday and I was late sending a present," she recalls. "I wanted to send a cake, but I couldn't find anyone to do it." One cake-sending service she found couldn't deliver the cake that day. And a local bakery wouldn't accept payment over the phone. Tsakoumakis decided that if no one else could provide nationwide cake delivery, she would do it herself. She already had toll-free telephone service and credit card accounts from a mail-order venture that flopped. All she needed was a system—and a lot of persistence.

"Trying to convince bakers that I was legitimate, that I wasn't trying to take their money, was the hardest part," Tsakoumakis says. "There was an organization before me that was doing a similar thing, but they went out of business and the bakers lost a lot of money. I had to convince them that I had nothing to do with them."

After she lined up the bakeries, delivery was sometimes a problem. "Bakeries are used to delivering big orders like wedding cakes," she explains. "But for small orders like mine, some of them didn't want to bother." When bakeries refuse to deliver, Tsakoumakis calls local delivery services or florists to do the job. In two years, she's had to turn away only three or four orders because she couldn't find vendors. Considering she processes some sixty-five orders a month, that's not a bad average.

Assembling a network of bakers is the biggest challenge Tsakoumakis has faced. Perhaps next in line is advertising. Because her market is nationwide—and her budget is not— getting the word out about HB Bakery Connection takes some creativity. "The main source of advertising is the bakers themselves," she says. "People will call them and say, 'I can't send a cake to someone in another city, can I?' They'll say, 'Yes, you can,' and give them my number." Tsakoumakis also distributes promotional posters to participating bakers and runs occasional ads in the local paper. She's had a lot of local and national publicity as well, including an article in *Family Circle* magazine.

"I could have put a lot of money into advertising right from the beginning, but I didn't have enough capital to do that," says Tsakoumakis. "I made a lot of mistakes in past businesses, so I was really cautious with this one. I didn't want to put so much money into this that, if it failed, I'd be out thousands of dollars."

If that growth hasn't been exactly explosive at HB Bakery Connection (Tsakoumakis is still her own lone employee), it's suited this owner just fine. Keeping the business manageable is one of her primary goals. Working at home enables her to spend time with her daughters Jennifer, 6, and Pamela, 4. "If I had grown too fast, I would have defeated my own purpose," she says. "I want to be their mother first." The slow, stable growth also allows her to learn as she goes. "Everything has gone along at a pace that I can handle," she stresses.

Certainly, the world is ready for services like these. Last

Mother's Day, Tsakoumakis ran an ad in the local paper and was deluged with calls. "I guess a lot of people don't live in the same towns as their mothers," she says. While Tsakoumakis wishes "good luck" to others interested in starting nation-wide cake-delivery services ("I know what it's like to convince these bakers"), the principle easily applies to other prod-ucts—gift baskets, restaurant gift certificates, and so on. All you need is a telephone, stationery, and the perseverance to see the business through its start-up.

Tsakoumakis encourages aspiring entrepreneurs to start their own businesses. Even the long hours and hard work that go into developing a new concept are worth the effort. "As long as you feel in your heart that a business will work, go for it," Tsakoumakis advises. "Otherwise, you'll sit on the fence for the rest of your life."

2

LIFE OF THE PARTY

BRIDAL CONSULTING

Business:

Planning, coordinating, and supervising weddings

Basic Equipment and Expenses:

$2,500

Necessities:

Telephone with answering service/machine, transportation, typewriter

Experience Required:

Familiarity with wedding etiquette, knowledge of local sites and vendors, ability to listen, nerves of steel

Inside Tip:

Consulting expert Gerard Monaghan suggests watching soap-opera weddings to keep abreast of the latest trends. What's hot this year? "Ultra-ultra elegance," he says.

As assistant buyer for a posh San Francisco department store, Janet Ellinwood saw her share of harried brides. One bride was so aggravated with her caterer that she contracted hives. "We had to cover a beautiful backless dress with a huge veil to hide the rash," Ellinwood recalls. "I thought, 'It shouldn't have to be this way.' And it doesn't."

That episode got Ellinwood thinking. She worked with scores of anxious brides who would gladly have paid someone else to coordinate their weddings. Ellinwood began reading up on the business of bridal consulting, and her suspicions were confirmed: Planning weddings was a viable business. In 1983, she opened The Carefree Bride.

"Basically, I take the pressure off the bride," Ellinwood explains. Her services vary from basic day-of-the-wedding supervision (for $800) to a complete ($2,500) package that includes finding a site; lining up caterers, musicians, photographers, florists, and transportation; printing and addressing the invitations; coordinating travel plans for out-of-town guests; running the wedding itself; and handling a host of other little decisions and crises.

Ellinwood describes her clientele as "thirty to forty-five years old and professional." Many are doctors, lawyers, and engineers. "These are people who don't have time to plan their own weddings," she says. "I've actually had clients write to me and say that if they hadn't hired me, they would have eloped."

Time is not the only savings, either. "Hiring a bridal consultant is beginning to be looked upon as money-saving as well," says Gerard Monaghan, president of the Association of Bridal Consultants in New Milford, Connecticut. "When a bride deals with a supplier, it's a one-shot deal. But when a consultant is involved, the supplier has the chance to get some repeat business. They're more likely to do a better job, and they are more likely to offer a discount. A consultant can get the bride the best possible wedding within her budget."

According to both Monaghan and Ellinwood, starting a wedding consultancy requires more time than money. Ellinwood launched her business from home with only a typewriter, a telephone, an answering machine, and some business cards. On the other hand, she estimates that a good two years passed before she established a regular stable of suppliers. Knowing quality suppliers, Ellinwood notes, is the key to her success. Similarly, Monaghan cautions new consultants against expecting too much too soon. A new consultant can turn a profit on his or her first wedding, but developing a steady, lucrative business can take as long as two to four years.

Ellinwood and Monaghan also emphasized the importance of people skills. Brides, Ellinwood points out, are under a lot of pressure. "You have to be a calming influence," she explains. "You have to really know what you're doing." Moreover, you have to be able to work effectively and harmoniously with a variety of vendors. A reputation for being difficult won't get you far in this business.

If there's one drawback to bridal consulting, it's long hours. The fifty to seventy weddings that Ellinwood plans each year keep her, her mother, and two employees hopping. Ellinwood herself works seven days a week. Yet, she notes that the rewards of her business outweigh the heavy workload. "I don't even realize the hours are long," she says, "because I love what I'm doing."

For More Information:

Association of Bridal Consultants
200 Chestnutland Road
New Milford, CT 06776-2521
(203) 355-0464

REUNION PLANNING

Business:

Planning and executing class reunions, includes everything from tracking down estranged classmates to coordinating vendors on the day of the party

Basic Equipment and Expenses:

$10,000

Necessities:

Telephone, transportation, home computer recommended

Experience Required:

Detective skills (must be able to locate long-lost classmates), organization, attention to detail; working within a tight budget is essential

Inside Tip:

A good reunion planner provides service above and beyond what an amateur planning committee could do itself. Take the time to develop professional methods—especially for locating attendees—before you launch your service.

"Anybody who's ever planned a reunion knows how many details go into it," says David Fiore, owner of Reunion Time, Inc. in Tinton Falls, New Jersey. "Trying to find people—even with their married names—coordinating vegetarian meals, dealing with special requests, lining up the caterers and the entertainment and sometimes limousines: It's a lot of details to keep straight."

These days, many reunion committees don't have the time to bother. They're busy managing careers and families.

Planning a successful reunion (i.e., one that brings together hundreds of long-lost friends) takes time and skill—of which the average person has neither. Yet most people look forward to their class reunions, anticipating them for years in advance.

"There are a lot of people who want to have class reunions, but don't have the time to plan them themselves," Fiore says. For this market, Reunion Time provides the following services:

1. Trying to locate everyone from a given class
2. Handling all communications—from invitations to reminder cards to telephone calls, and so on
3. Keeping accurate records of all expenses
4. Lining up vendors (caterers, entertainment, decorators, hotel accommodations, photographers, etc.).

This includes signing contracts and paying vendors their deposits up front. Normally, the planning committee would put up this money, which sometimes totals as much as $2,000 to $3,000. "We take some of the risks out of planning a reunion," says Fiore.

For the planning committee, Fiore's service is a true bargain. Because Reunion Time's operations are so efficient, the price of a planned reunion is no higher than what a committee might pay if they handled it themselves.

Fiore started the business with partner Bonnie Burt in 1985 (Burt is now also his wife). Both were working for a major corporation when they caught the entrepreneurial bug. "I'd had my own businesses since I was thirteen," Fiore explains. "I heard about other people doing reunion planning and thought it was a good idea." To learn more about the business, Fiore "crashed a lot of other people's reunions." From that, he got a sense of what worked and what didn't. Then he and Burt started planning in earnest, developing a system that was both effective and efficient.

"This is not a high-margin business," says Fiore. "You don't make a lot of money unless you're really efficient, because you can only charge so much for your services." In addition to being efficient, Fiore also recommends providing value. "In real estate, it's location, location, location," he says. "In this business, it's turnout, turnout, turnout." Going the extra mile to find and recruit participants is critical. To that end, Reunion Time employs some 100 people, the bulk of whom do part-time research from their homes.

Reunion Time doesn't do any advertising. Referrals from past attendees—as well as high schools and vendors—give them more than enough business. This year, Reunion Time expects to plan over 300 reunions.

While start-up costs for equipment and facilities are relatively low in this business, Fiore emphasizes that skill and planning requirements are high. "Some people think just anyone can call themselves a reunion planner and get into this business, but it isn't that easy," he says. "You have to be organized, and you have to be willing to put in hard work. We work sixteen-hour days, seven days a week to provide quality service."

CATERING

Business:

Supplying food to parties, corporate events, weddings, etc.

Basic Equipment and Expenses:

$2,500

Necessities:

Transportation, preferably a station wagon or van large enough to carry equipment to various sites; depending on state and local regulations on cooking at home, most caterers rent kitchen facilities

Experience Required:

None, but having worked for a caterer in the past—even briefly—helps tremendously

Inside Tip:

Don't quit your day job. According to National Caterer's Association president Tony Rubino, it can take as long as three to five years to establish a steady catering business. He advises keeping your regular job during the week and catering evenings and weekends to start.

Catering is currently the fastest-growing segment of the food service industry, Tony Rubino says. Why? "For people who are interested in food service, catering is the easiest field to jump into," Rubino says. Unlike starting a restaurant, launching a catering company doesn't require that you lease a location, hire a permanent staff, or even buy equipment. "You can start a catering business for $500, depending on the circumstances and what you want to do," says Rubino.

As leisure time gets scarcer and tastes become more sophisticated, the catering business gets ever more popular. Not only are caterers *de rigueur* at weddings these days, but they're also showing up at corporate meetings, company picnics, grand-opening celebrations, private parties—just about everywhere that food can be served. Small wonder that catering is a $6 billion industry.

While it's possible to spend a small fortune launching your own catering company, it's also common to start on a shoestring. The biggest variables are location and equipment. If you're catering off-premise (at your clients' locations), you may be able to prepare the food on their premises, thereby eliminating the need for your own kitchen. Since this can be a little limiting, you may also want to consider renting a health-licensed kitchen on a per-use basis from a local restaurant or church. Equipment, too, may be rented. Everything from chafing dishes to linen tablecloths are available from your local party rental company.

To succeed at catering, you should be able to cook. But the simple preparation of edibles isn't all in this business. "The food has to be good," says Mark Fahrer, a New York caterer with over $2 million in annual sales, "but catering is more than just food on a plate. Catering is a bigger beast." Finding sites, working with decorators, staying within a budget, dreaming up themes—these are all part and parcel of the caterer's trade.

Establishing yourself in the catering business can take time if your funds are limited—often three to five years to get themselves up and running at full capacity. Once you are established, there are several opportunities for expansion. One is to find yourself a site. Joyce Wilson Neil of Party Time Catering in San Pablo, California, runs her catering service from a former Rockefeller hunting lodge. "People are desperate for locations," she reports. Another idea is to expand your services into party planning. The contacts you make as a caterer could be your entrée into more comprehensive services.

For More Information:

National Caterer's Association
220 South State Street, Suite 1416
Chicago, IL 60604-2198
800-848-3663

MOBILE DISK JOCKEY SERVICE

Business:

Providing the music for weddings, parties, and other private affairs

Basic Equipment and Expenses:

$7,500

Necessities:

Telephone, transportation, stereo sound system, large record collection

Experience Required:

Must be reliable, personable, and knowledgeable about music

Inside Tip:

Start out by pricing your services low. While advertising is possible, networking at the jobs themselves leads to the most business. Putting in the lowest bid will help you land your first jobs.

Music may have charms to soothe the savage beast—but it can also make or break a party. That's why people around the country hire mobile disk jockeys to spin records at weddings, parties, and other special events. As New York mobile DJ Stuart Cohen puts it, "We provide music and personalities for birthday parties, weddings, bar mitzvahs, graduation parties—at private homes, in catering halls, on boats. We do it all."

Cohen launched his company, Sounds Great Systems, in college on an initial investment of $3,000. "I bought some basic equipment and a small record collection and put on a 'Pub Night' in the campus pub," he says. Cohen furnished more than just music: He also hosted limbo contests and "Name That Tune" segments. In time, he was invited to work fraternity and sorority parties, and the business snowballed from there.

Cohen reports that personality is as important as the music itself in this business. "You have to know when to talk and when to shut up," he says. "You have to have a good time and move around and clap your hands and motivate people. You have to be able to read a crowd, to know what song is going to get them off their behinds and onto the dance floor."

The musical aspect of the business is also important, of course. To get started in this business, you need a good basic sound system and a large, diverse selection of music. You'll save substantially on start-up costs if you already own a big record collection. Having the latest tunes is vital, and so is having plenty of old standards. Says Cohen, "You have to have every song a client requests." Over the years, Cohen has accumulated quite an assortment of records—from ethnic songs to torch songs from the thirties and forties.

The hours in this business can work with or against you. If you're just starting out, working weekends and evenings will enable you to hold on to your job while you're getting established. For Cohen, the hours that agreed with his college lifestyle don't suit his newly married existence. Through more aggressive marketing, he believes he could bring in more-than-full-time earnings. But because he wants to spend time with his wife and family, he works days as a marketing manager and keeps his music business strictly part time. Even so, the profits are enviable. At $400 for an average four-hour job—and bookings for four parties a weekend—the business is thriving even part time.

LIFE OF THE PARTY

> Jan Parrott started The Particular Parrott with only a little experience, a few contacts, and business cards she colored herself. Today, her home-based event-planning firm grosses $800,000 a year.

Laguna Beach, California, entrepreneur Jan Parrott didn't have the benefit of a role model. When she started The Particular Parrott in 1979, she wasn't even sure that event planning was a business. But in her work for a local catering company, she noticed a need. The executive secretaries usually called upon to handle parties and special events were too busy to do a good job.

"I drew a parrot of my own design and took it to the print shop to have cards printed up," Parrott recalls. "Then I colored in the parrots myself with a magic marker. With my heart pounding, I went to some of my old contacts and said, 'Look, I don't know if you need any services like these, but this is what I'm planning to do.' Talk about the positive approach to starting a business."

Positive or not, Parrott landed projects. "I was averaging about one party every six months in the beginning," she says. "But I made more money doing that than I did working full time." Since then, the business has grown a respectable 33 percent annually. Today, The Particular Parrott bills $800,000 a year.

It all started with catering. Parrott, a former elementary school teacher, started working for a local caterer while her children were small. "I discovered you could make a lot of money spooning peas," she jokes. She developed such a knack for the business that she became the sales manager—and a good one at that.

But Parrott wasn't comfortable working for someone else. "I would go out and sell a party and when the day of the party came around, the owner would change the menu or cut corners. I felt terrible about it," Parrott says. "I was working long hours and feeling unappreciated, and very responsible for a company that wasn't even mine."

But if her catering job wasn't the career of a lifetime, it did teach Parrott a thing or two about business. "I learned where to get things, how much to charge. I discovered the principle that it's not how much something is worth, but how much a customer perceives it's worth." And she made contacts—the same contacts that led to her first accounts.

Most of Parrott's business is corporate. She handles events for advertising agencies, orchestrates grand openings and open houses for local developers. Though she points out that many society functions pay as well as corporate events, Parrott prefers working with businesses. "Corporate accounts do parties more regularly," she says. "And I don't have to deal with all the things that can make this job awful—fighting and last-minute changes and so on." Her budgets range from $3,000 to $60,000, with $18,000 to $35,000 being the average. Profits range from 15 to 35 percent.

To succeed as an event planner, Parrott believes you must be organized, creative, and intuitive—and keep those three elements in constant balance. You do not have to be a fabulous cook or a brilliant decorator, though it helps to have enough taste to spot competence in others. "Probably the biggest challenge for me is keeping fresh," she says. "It would be easy for me to just stay in the same niche, to keep doing the same party over and over again. But it's important to me to get out and see what other people are doing and think about new possibilities.

"Also, being a single woman in business, with no board of directors and no one to tell me what I should be doing, it can be hard to keep the focus," she continues. "But I want to keep this business small. I don't want the responsibility of having a lot of overhead and hiring employees."

On the other hand, Parrott has contemplated additional projects. Helping two women in Denver launch their event planning service got her thinking about franchising. "I've thought about it," she says, "but the spiritual side of me is very important. I don't want to lose my time to myself." She would also like to sponsor seminars for aspiring women entrepreneurs. "I'd like to tell them that if you want to do something, you don't look outside yourself: you look inside."

To those of you who want to become event planners, Parrott advises learning the business from the inside. "It's better to just go in, roll up your sleeves, and start working on the low end for a caterer," she says. "You'll learn what foods will work in various situations, what can and can't be done. It's important to know all those things once you become a planner, so you don't ask people to do the impossible."

A CLEAN SWEEP

Window Cleaning Service

Business:

Cleaning windows for both residential and commercial clients

Basic Equipment and Expenses:

$4,500

Necessities:

Bucket, squeegee, cleaning solution, ladder, poles, rags, transportation, telephone

Experience Required:

None

Inside Tip:

Staying lean and mean will help you get your foot in the door. Contracts tend to go to the lowest bidder, so keep your operations efficient.

Let other cleaning services say they don't do windows: Window cleaning in and of itself is a viable, profitable business. And the market is by no means limited to disgruntled housewives. In fact, most of the money in this business is made cleaning windows on storefronts and commercial buildings. With little more than a bucket and a squeegee, you can put yourself in business.

But starting out small doesn't necessarily mean staying that way. Stan Ehrenkranz of Texas Window Cleaning in Houston reports gross annual sales of $500,000. When Stan's father bought the company in 1949, it was a floundering firm. Over the years, sound management and a solid reputation has turned Texas Window Cleaning into one of the area's most established window cleaning services.

Texas Window Cleaning does mostly commercial cleaning, including work on local skyscrapers. Because of high insurance and workman's compensation costs, Ehrenkranz doesn't recommend starting out in this area. "Our biggest problem is insurance and workman's comp," he says. Safety, too, is a major concern. "We try not to have any injuries at all, to avoid any kinds of accidents," he continues. "One bad accident could put us out of business." While expanding into this kind of work may be a lucrative down-the-road move, it's risky on a shoestring budget. This is one case where cheap, faulty equipment just won't do.

If there's a market in your area for a window cleaning service, your determination—and not prior experience—will make the difference between success and failure, Ehrenkranz says. He took over his business ten years ago when his father died unexpectedly. "I didn't know much," he recalls, but inexperience didn't kill the business. "In fact, we were making more money when I didn't know anything," he jokes. "That was more a function of the economy here in

Houston taking a downturn recently, but it does tell you something."

MAID SERVICE

Business:

Dusting, vacuuming, sweeping, mopping, and—yes—doing windows

Basic Equipment and Expenses:

$2,500

Necessities:

Basic cleaning equipment and supplies, transportation, telephone

Experience Required:

Professional cleaning experience helpful, though it's possible to hire experienced people and leave the cleaning to them

Inside Tip:

A hidden source of one-time business is in new homes. Clean up new houses for their new owners before they move in. An added bonus: They may become regular clients after they're settled.

Armed with $700 and 20,000 flyers, former clerical worker Christi Spruill started Good Housekeepers, Inc. in 1983 in the Houston suburb of Spring. Why? "I just had an idea that a maid service would be good in this area," Spruill says. "I thought Houston needed one."

If the 100-plus homes Good Housekeepers cleans a week are any evidence, Spruill was right. Dual-income professionals comprise most of Good Housekeepers' market. In the past year, business has doubled at Spruill's firm. And as Houston's economy continues to recover from the recent oil glut, growth for services like Good Housekeepers is due to quicken.

Inexperience is no excuse for not starting a maid service. Do you hate selling? Spruill hired students to distribute flyers door to door in some of the more upscale neighborhoods in town. Now, advertising by direct mail and coupon books do the selling for her. Are you a poor housekeeper? Many maid service owners never push a broom or wring a mop. Hiring experienced cleaning people will increase your potential volume. And if you've never cleaned professionally, an experienced crew can probably clean rings around you anyway.

You don't need experience to succeed in the cleaning business, but you do need people skills. Providing excellent customer service is essential, both in keeping your current accounts and encouraging referrals. "Be up-front and honest," Spruill advises. "When you look at a problem, imagine yourself on the other side, and treat that person the way you'd want to be treated." You must also be able to manage a large, independent staff. "Every day, someone calls in to say their child is sick or their car won't start or something," says Spruill. "You have to be patient," she continues, and you have to be prepared with a backup crew.

"Anybody's capable of doing what I've done," says Spruill. "All you need is to do good work and market your business properly."

JANITORIAL SERVICE

Business:

Cleaning office and commercial buildings

Basic Equipment and Expenses:

$3,000

Necessities:

Telephone, transportation, broom, mop, vacuum, cleaning supplies

Experience Required:

None

Inside Tip:

Be prepared for long hours in this business. In the beginning, you may have to spend all day on marketing and administration, then clean a full shift at night.

With over 35,000 janitorial services in the United States, the janitorial industry grosses about $10.2 billion in annual sales and employs some six million people. The janitorial business also represents one of the simplest businesses an entrepreneur can get into. Basically, all you need is cleaning equipment and salesmanship.

"It's really easy," reports Ron Muir of Affordable Maintenance in Seattle, Washington. "You go out and pound the pavement with some business cards." That isn't to say it isn't hard work: Direct selling is inexpensive, but it takes time and effort. "It's a numbers game," Muir reports. "A lot of people don't know how to sell. They can't take rejection. You have to make about fifty contacts to get one account."

The business itself is straightforward: cleaning commercial properties after hours. You can do the work yourself, or hire a crew to handle it. Working alone, Muir estimates that you can make $20 to $30 an hour. With a crew, your margin drops but your volume rises. With the help of six employees, Muir cleans ten buildings regularly—some weekly, some nightly. "As an owner without a night manager, that's about as big as you can get comfortably," he says.

Muir warns that if you're serious about the janitorial business, you should be prepared to wear a lot of hats. Beyond the cleaning, there's plenty of marketing, accounting, customer service, and management to be done. Long hours and multiple duties make burnout a constant danger. "I would suggest finding a very dependable partner to share some of the work," says Muir, "or finding someone to take some of the night work off your hands, as soon as the business can afford it."

CARPET CLEANING

Business:

Commercial and residential carpet cleaning

Basic Equipment and Expenses:

$5,000

Necessities:

Carpet cleaning equipment, spot-removing chemicals, telephone, transportation

Experience Required:

None

Inside Tip:

Expand into other areas of cleaning as your business grows. If you can't fund the expansion yourself, carpet cleaner Bill Secolo suggests contracting out new services at first.

Most people know that carpet cleaning is a relatively stable industry. As long as carpets get dirty, carpet cleaning services will flourish. But many people do not know that it's also fun—at least according to Seattle carpet cleaner Bill Secolo. Secolo left a good job in the aeronautics industry to run his own carpet cleaning business. Why? "This may sound funny, but I cleaned carpets to put myself through school and I really enjoyed it," he says. "Finally, I decided I enjoyed it more than my work [in the aviation industry]."

According to Secolo, there's more to carpet cleaning than simple steam and suds. Applying his scientific mind to the process, he's come up with remedies for common carpet stains using everyday household products. He has also pioneered some new carpet dyeing technologies, including spot dyeing, fade restoration, and dye lot matching.

In terms of innovation, Secolo believes he took his cue from his former employer. "They were the best in the aviation industry," he says, "and one reason was the testing they did. When I worked there, I thought testing was a waste of dollars, but now I see what they were doing. When you try new things, you're not going to make a profit on every job. But what you learn may enable you to earn money down the road."

Since he started the business in 1980, Secolo has certainly lived up to that philosophy. He entered the business with used equipment he rehabilitated himself. "I think I spent about $500," he says. "But then, I didn't have any more than that to spend." He moonlighted until his nighttime earnings matched his daytime salary—about a year and a half.

Secolo says that a commitment to customer service has been his most important ally. "I tell my customers that I'm not the greatest guy in the world—in fact, there's a lot I don't know," he says. "But if they're ever unhappy with my service, they don't have to pay. Out of over five thousand customers, I haven't had more than three complaints. I established a good name for myself."

That good name got Secolo further than he originally planned. The more carpet cleaning he did, the more frequently he heard complaints about janitorial services. Finally, one of his clients—a major software manufacturer—asked if he wouldn't like a shot at declined janitorial work as well. Since he knew nothing about the janitorial business, he hired Seattle consultant William Griffin to teach him the tricks of the cleaning trade. A few weeks later, he found himself in the janitorial business. Now, janitorial work makes up about 60 percent of sales at Secolo's firm, Superior Cleaning Services—sales that in 1988 reached $1.2 million.

Part of Secolo's secret has been specialization. While it might seem that the type of office would have nothing to do with the cleaning involved, Secolo's high-tech clients prove otherwise. "At many companies, employees are expected to do a lot of their own janitorial work—clearing their desks or keeping their areas neat. Computer companies have a more college-campus environment," says Secolo. "They have a laid-back atmosphere." As a result, there is not only more mess, but more stains in the carpet. Secolo says his twin services are the perfect tie-ins. "I'm able to get the stains out of the carpet before the client even sees them," he says. That flexibility has been crucial. "If I had an ironclad system that I wanted to impose on them, I probably would never have gotten the account," he says.

Secolo also has a last word of advice for would-be cleaning professionals. You don't need unlimited funds to expand. If you're in one area of cleaning and have the opportunity to branch out into another, don't rely on your bank for help. Secolo's bank refused to boost his line of credit even though he already had a lucrative janitorial account. Instead, use subcontractors to get the service off the ground. Be honest: Tell them you only want their help until you can bring those services in-house, but that you can send some business their way until that time. This will enable you to offer a new service without buying new equipment or bankrolling a large payroll.

CEILING CLEANING SERVICE

Business:

Cleaning commercial and industrial ceilings with high-pressure equipment

Basic Equipment and Expenses:

$10,000

Necessities:

Telephone, transportation, ceiling-cleaning equipment

Experience Required:

Marketing and sales ability a must

Inside Tip:

In selling to commercial and industrial accounts, Ceiling Doctor Kaaydah Schatten notes that money is the biggest factor. "In the commercial market, the only thing that sells people is profits. The cost of replacing a ceiling is $2 per square foot. The cost of cleaning is about 20 cents per square foot. If you can save them money, they're interested."

"The next time you're in an office or industrial building, look up," urges Kaaydah Schatten of Ceiling Doctor International, Inc. in Toronto, Canada. "Ceilings get dirty—dirtier than carpets because hot air rises and takes pollution and smoke and bacteria with it. Most ceilings are filthy."

Schatten is no stranger to filthy ceilings. In fact, personal experience prompted Schatten to get into the business in the first place. "When I was younger, I used to renovate houses and I always had to tear out the ceiling," she says. "At that time, I thought, 'If someone could figure out how to clean a ceiling, they'd make a million dollars.'"

Not one to wait around for solutions, Schatten figured out the process herself. Schatten notes that ceiling cleaning is not a new business, rather one she feels she's refined to a science. She created four different equipment prototypes before she hit upon one that worked to her satisfaction. Now, her high-pressure, dry chemical ceiling cleaning equipment is used by Ceiling Doctor franchises across Canada and in the United States and Japan.

Today, commercial and industrial accounts comprise most of the business for ceiling cleaners. Manufacturing plants, restaurants, and office towers are just some of the locations that the Ceiling Doctor services. In the future, Schatten hopes to open up the residential market as well. "Commercial acceptance comes first," she says. "It's just like carpet cleaning: They went into the commercial market first. Now, everyone gets their carpets cleaned."

GREAT OUTDOORS

> Brian Winch started a janitorial business, but couldn't land any accounts. Then a building manager suggested he take his cleaning service outside—and he's been profitable ever since.

It was 1981, and Brian Winch was tired of his job. So he decided to start a cleaning service. But when he tried to drum up business for his janitorial service around Calgary,

Canada, he found the going tough. "It was extremely competitive up here," he reports. "Anyone with $100 can buy a couple of mops, a broom, and a used vacuum cleaner and get started in the janitorial business. That was easy; the hard part was getting a contract."

Then by chance he called the manager of a commercial strip center to inquire about bidding on the cleaning contract. "The guy told me he already had someone servicing the inside of the building, but that he was having a heck of a time finding someone to clean the outside of the building," says Winch. He volunteered his services on the spot, and Quality Maintenance was born.

Winch's service is basic: He removes litter from parking lots and landscaped areas. "You just walk around with a broom and a little scooper and remove trash," he says. "It's just like taking a walk." These skills were easy enough to acquire. Yet Winch has little competition even today. Within a month of landing that first contract, he had several others with the same manager. Today, he does over $60,000 in business by providing his own outdoor clean-up services and subcontracting out other types of outdoor maintenance like parking-lot sweeping, parking-lot striping, landscape maintenance, and snow removal.

For Winch, subcontracting has been a real boon. "At some point we realized that there were only so many buildings and so many services we could do without buying more equipment and renting bigger space and hiring more employees," he says. Yet the opportunity was there. Through contracting, Winch provides his customers with the services they want, boosts his own sales, and helps fellow business owners win new accounts.

Winch is so enthusiastic about the business that he's written a book on the subject. His creation, *Cleaning Up for Cash*, provides would-be maintenance brokers with valuable information on starting and running a service like Winch's. "It dumbfounds me that more people don't get into this business," he says. "It's an ideal business for students and part-

timers—or for people like me who just want their own businesses. There's very little competition in this field. You aren't
just another janitorial service going door to door. You have to
go out and get the accounts, but once you do that, all you
have to do is a good job."

4

MEDIA BLITZ

COMMERCIAL FREE-LANCE WRITING

Business:

Writing copy for ads, brochures, direct-mail pieces, corporate videos; also, free-lance writing for magazines, book publishers, newspapers, etc.

Basic Equipment and Expenses:

$3,500

Necessities:

Home computer with a printer, telephone, stationery

Experience Required:

Portfolio and/or clips of past work essential in landing new assignments, prior experience with an advertising agency or in an editorial office invaluable

Inside Tip:

Break into professional writing on your off-hours. Writing articles for your local paper or producing brochures for friends and relatives in business are a few outlets for beginners to try.

Yes, you can make a living as a free-lance writer—and you don't have to follow in the footsteps of Danielle Steel or Sidney Sheldon to do it. Today, good writers are in demand—not only for magazine work, books, and newspaper reporting, but also for advertising copy, direct-mail pieces, and training manuals.

Starting a free-lance writing business is as simple as buying a computer and setting up a desk. You don't need a lot of capital to start. However, you do need demonstrable experience. Getting your foot in the creative door is the first—and perhaps most difficult—step toward becoming a successful free-lancer.

Los Angeles-based copywriter Jerry Fisher's first advertising job was as a gofer. Once he was in the door, "I basically begged people to let me write some ads." he says. His work was good enough to move him up the corporate ladder. He became a copywriter, then creative supervisor, then creative director. Fisher's various positions gave him a wealth of experience in all phases of advertising—and the impressive portfolio of ads that helped him prove his abilities to future clients.

"The scary part at first is being cut off from a regular paycheck," Fisher says. "Initially, you really have to get out there and make yourself known." Once you do establish a steady clientele, however, you can bring in a sizable income. Fisher bills about $100,000 a year with only minimal marketing. "If I did more marketing, I think I'd have more work than I could handle," he explains.

Fisher recommends that aspiring writers develop their skills first, then contemplate free-lancing. Working for yourself, he reports, is more demanding than being an employee.

"As an employee, you can flub up now and then, and still get paid," he says. "As a free-lancer, you have to turn in great work, or you don't get paid. And you have to stay on the good side of your clients, because you don't survive in this business on one-shot assignments."

On the other hand, free-lancing allows Fisher to make a comfortable living on his own terms. "As a creative director, I got into more administrative and managerial work, and I didn't have the stomach for it," he says. "But to make good money at an agency, you have to be a manager. I realized that if I wanted to make the money, I had to free-lance."

Happily, the greatest challenge Fisher faces in his business is "deciding how much business I can take in and still maintain a high level of quality. You never want to say 'no,' but often you have so much work on your plate that you can't handle any more."

VIDEOTAPING SERVICE

Business:

Videotaping weddings, parties, bar mitzvahs, legal contract proceedings, Little League games, family histories, training films, video résumés, etc.

Basic Equipment and Expenses:

$4,500

Necessities:

Telephone, transportation, camcorder, various accessories (many of which may be available through a rental company)

Experience Required:

Facility with videotaping and editing equipment necessary; since a good part of this business involves attending other people's parties, people skills also vital

Inside Tip:

Think creatively. While the videotaping business isn't new, new applications are being dreamed up daily. The more resourceful you are, the bigger your business will be.

Once upon a time, seeing yourself on television was a momentous, once-in-a-lifetime event—worthy of phone calls to all your friends and relatives, and maybe a few rivals.

Today, being on television is still momentous. But thanks to the growing number of videotaping firms around the country, it's no longer a once-in-a-lifetime event. What was the exclusive domain of photographers is now fertile ground for videotaping services.

Randy Moss, founder of RAM Video Production in Tarzana, California, brings in over $100,000 a year taping weddings, bar mitzvahs, and legal contract proceedings, as well as commercial and industrial videos. With just a little practice and a video camera he borrowed from his brother, Moss developed enough skill to launch his business.

Moss started the business out in an apartment, but eventually upgraded both his business location and his residence. Now, he lives in a house and works out of a studio that's located near a bridal shop, a tuxedo-rental store, and a wedding photographer—all ample sources of walk-in business. Moss doesn't spend much money on advertising. Instead, he relies on quality work and reliable service to bring in referrals.

"Since this is a totally people-oriented business, you really have to cater to your clients," Moss says. "And since we don't advertise, we can't progress [without word of mouth from satisfied customers]."

Breaking into the video business is relatively simple. The

basic skills you'll need as a videographer can be mastered at home, or in night school or extension courses. Videotaping equipment is getting better every day—a good camcorder can be bought for less than $3,000. Landing your first few accounts is probably the biggest hurdle. Calling on friends and simply going door to door seems to be the commonest way to get a business going.

In the past few years, the videotaping business has become increasingly diverse. Among the innovations we've seen: video family albums, video résumés, video press releases, industrial training videos, video greeting cards—the list goes on and on. With a little ingenuity, the possibilities are virtually limitless.

GRAPHIC DESIGN

Business:

Designing books, magazines, brochures, advertisements, and other printed matter

Basic Equipment and Expenses:

$5,000

Necessities:

Drafting table, art supplies, telephone, letterhead, advertising, computer for desktop publishing (optional)

Experience Required:

Must know design and production techniques, either through classes or hands-on experience

Inside Tip:

If you don't already have a portfolio of samples, start one now. Create sample projects if you don't have any suitable work to show.

Thumb through just about any magazine on the newsstand and you'll see how graphically sophisticated Americans have become. Creative layouts, slick photography, and eye-catching colors aren't outstanding anymore—they're common. And magazines are only an indicator. In print ads, packaging, flyers, and business stationery, professional-looking graphics can make or break a company's image.

Even small companies are living up to higher standards of graphic excellence. One of the first expenses meeting-planner Shirley Marley incurred in her new business was printing and production of a promotional mail piece. "I had it professionally done," Marley says, "because it was important that my company look good to potential clients."

The demand for professional graphic services is on the rise, and small firms are taking up the slack. "As advertising agencies got bigger and bigger, I saw that a lot of small- to medium-sized companies weren't getting the attention they wanted," says Cathy Lentz of Designed Response, a marketing design firm in San Clemente, California. "We bill ourselves as an alternative to an ad agency. We're different in that we don't book media, there's no retainer, we work on a project-by-project basis, and we involve our clients in the creative process. Entrepreneurial people seem to like the control."

Lentz started out with $10,000 in working capital. In addition to basic equipment and supplies, she used those funds to keep herself afloat as she built the business. Working alone, she spent her days fielding phone calls and going out to make presentations, then returning home at four o'clock to start her "real work." On the other hand, Designed Response grossed $60,000 in its first year, 1986. In the first quarter of 1989, it billed $200,000.

Lentz credits her success to a good education and a strong creative sense. A graphic arts degree from the University of California and production experience on regional magazines gave her a solid background for this business. But Lentz points out that a four-year degree isn't the only way to break into the field. "It's possible to learn how to do what we're doing by working under someone who's experienced," she says, "as long as you can work with someone who's really knowledgeable." You may also assign some tasks to free-lancers, though doing so cuts into your bottom line.

Generally speaking, this is not a business for the graph-ically illiterate. Lentz stresses that staying on top of the latest design trends is critical. "You have to know what companies want from people in your field," she says. "We're constantly keeping up with what's happening in the market, and we're always trying to outdo what we've done before. Most of our business comes through referrals, and we've never lost a client. I think that's because we maintain very high stan-dards."

NEWSLETTER PUBLISHING

Business:

Creating, publishing, and distributing newsletters, either independently or for corporations, nonprofit groups, etc.

Basic Equipment and Expenses:

$10,000

Necessities:

Computer (desktop publishing software optional), pasteup supplies, telephone

Experience Required:

Must be familiar with any or all of the following: writing, graphic design, desktop publishing, printing, newsletter marketing—or must have special, marketable area of expertise

Inside Tip:

Write what you know. Focusing on a subject you're familiar with and like will make you a better writer and editor—and increase your chances of success.

One of the casualties of fast-paced living is reading time. Most of us are happy just to get through the morning paper. There are hundreds of specialized topics that people need information on, but most of us don't have the time to scan trade journals, pore over reference books, or catch up on the latest studies. Fast information is at a premium, and newsletter publishers around the country are addressing the demand.

Cindy Ware of Acton, Massachusetts, is one such publisher. Frustrated by the lack of accessible information on summer programs for junior-high and high-school students, Ware decided to publish a newsletter on the subject. The result is a ten-volume compendium of summer programs for teens called *Exploroptions*. The listings are divided into categories like "Archaeology and Anthropology" and "Outdoor Adventures."

"There are so many negatives out there for kids," says Ware. "We're always saying, 'Don't do drugs' or 'don't break the law.' But we have to offer some positive alternatives. For many kids, school is not a positive experience. Summer programs can make a difference. They can break that cycle of poor self-esteem." According to Ware, there's a wealth of interesting programs available to teens, including vocational and travel-abroad programs. The problem was, they had no easy way to find out about them. Now, Ware's *Exploroptions* reaches junior-high and high-school guidance counselors around the country.

On a different note, retired history professor Don Johnson publishes a newsletter on the stock market out of his spare bedroom in Santa Rosa, California. His *On-Line Investment Letter* offers stock tips to investors who don't have time to follow the market. Johnson recently acquired his SEC license and spends about twenty hours a week at the library researching companies. After playing the stock market for twenty-three years, keeping track of market trends is practically second nature to Johnson, who is glad to have "something to do" in his retirement.

These are literally two ideas out of thousands. Newsletters exist on all varieties of subjects, from analysis of major industries to tips on local gardening. Independent newsletters aren't the only option, either. Businesses, shops, hospitals, dentists, car dealerships, nonprofit groups—all kinds of organizations use newsletters to keep customers up-to-date and informed on new products and services.

Costs for starting a newsletter vary considerably. Ware's project cost roughly $15,000 to start, including her Macintosh computer with desktop publishing software and a laser printer. Other major expenses included gathering information (she mailed detailed questionnaires to hundreds of companies) and direct-mail marketing of the finished product. These expenses were critical to Ware, who felt that comprehensive information and a good presentation were essential. You may be able to save on your start-up expenses by economizing on equipment and/or research. For instance, producing a gardening newsletter for your local nursery would entail none of the mailing and marketing costs that Ware had.

On the other hand, Ware's investment has paid off. Recently, an educational publisher agreed to feature the ten-volume set of *Exploroptions* in their upcoming catalog. She has also been approached by a major book publisher to create a directory from the information she's compiled. Ware is delighted with her success—especially all the good her

work has accomplished. "There are so many wonderful programs available to kids," she says. "You can do anything you
want as a teenager." Thanks to Ware's work, more and more
people are realizing that.

SELF-PUBLISHING

Business:

Writing, printing, and marketing your own books

Basic Equipment and Expenses:

$10,000

Necessities:

Word processor, basic office equipment (desk, chair, etc.),
phone

Experience Required:

No specific requirements; writing skill, marketing ability,
and/or a good idea are good starting points

Inside Tip:

The mailing lists you compile for book marketing may be
valuable to other businesses. Rent out your mailing list for
additional profits.

Some people wait their whole lives for a publisher's acceptance letter. If you have a book idea that you think will
sell, why not publish it yourself and keep the profits? According to Santa Barbara, California, self-publisher Dan Poynter,
you don't need to write like Hemingway to produce a suc-

cessful book. In fact, any number of tasks—from writing to editing to marketing—can be handled by other people.

Every good book starts with an idea. What do you know that other people want to find out? Maybe you're an expert on housebreaking rabbits. Or perhaps you have a collection of job-winning résumés. Poynter knew plenty about parachuting. Having been a parachute designer for years, he knew the ins and outs of the subject—and he knew that no comprehensive manual had been published on it. In 1969, he sat down to write.

That book was so successful that Poynter started shopping for additional ideas. In 1973, hang-gliding was starting to catch on. He spent three months writing all about hang-gliding, and sold enough books on that subject to buy himself a house in Santa Barbara. One of the advantages of self-publishing, according to Poynter, is speed. "It took me about five months to write and print my hang-gliding book," he says. "A regular book publisher takes eighteen months. I sold 50,000 copies by the time any other publisher came out with a book on the same subject."

Breaking into the publishing business is easier than you might think. If you plan to write your own book, you'll need a computer to handle word processing. This will come in handy when you do direct mailings as well. As an option, you might want to consider buying a complete desktop publishing system—with publishing software and a laser printer. Though this will cost you considerably more, it may save you time and money in typesetting costs.

"I like to overestimate a little bit and say it takes $12,000 to publish a book," says Poynter. The printing bill for 3,000 copies of a typical book is only $4,000 to $5,000. But, Poynter notes, the costs of pre-printing production and promotion add up, and you'll need some means of support while you're putting it all together. Poynter does agree that it is possible to publish a book for less than $10,000 though, if you're careful about costs.

Poynter also warns would-be publishers not to let little obstacles get in their way. If you don't know how to type, for instance, you can dictate your book into a tape recorder and have a word-processing service prepare it for you. That way, you save the cost of a computer as well. If you've never seen a book on your topic in a bookstore, don't despair: Rejoice. Alternative marketing through direct mail and targeted ads may reach your untapped market more effectively than a bookstore can. Even if your expertise is a little shaky, you can make sure your facts are straight by sending it out to experts for review. "We try to impress upon people that you can work with other people," says Poynter. "In fact, it's usually a good idea."

To get more information about self-publishing, Poynter recommends networking with other publishers. "Book publishers are usually very helpful because very few books compete directly with other books," he says. "As long as you're not a direct competitor, they're happy to give you information."

For More Information:

Para Publishing
Post Office Box 4232-882
Santa Barbara, California 93140
Free brochure on Para Publishing's guides to producing and marketing books

CARTOON MAP PUBLISHING

Business:

Publishing cartoon maps of your hometown. Businesses pay to put themselves on the map

Basic Equipment and Expenses:

$8,500

Necessities:

Telephone, brochures, sample maps, business cards

Experience Required:

Sales experience most necessary, other tasks can be contracted out

Inside Tip:

Consider other novel ways to tap into your local market for print ads. How about publishing a calendar of local events? A cookbook of menus—or recipes—from local restaurants?

Tempe, Arizona, entrepreneurs Jack Eddy and Ron Beckman have an unusual approach to local directory publishing. Instead of putting out a new version of the Yellow Pages, they squeeze a book full of information onto a page—in map form. For the two founders of Fiesta Cartoon Maps, cartoon cartography represents hundreds of thousands in sales annually through their nationwide network of licensees.

Eddy and Beckman got into the map business quite by accident. It was 1979, and the partners were marketing sports posters for professional basketball and football teams, for bowl games, and for Arizona State University sports. The partners made their money from ads printed at the bottoms of the posters. As a favor, ASU asked the partners if they could help the varsity club raise a little extra money. Beckman proposed selling ads on a cartoon map of ASU's hometown, Tempe.

"We sold ads for two hundred dollars each and made thousands of dollars for the varsity club," says Beckman. "ASU wasn't interested the next year, so we did the Tempe map for ourselves."

The maps are as fun to read as they are clever. Strict geographical accuracy isn't a priority. Instead, the maps emphasize whimsy. They are not drawn to scale, but participating businesses are placed in their correct areas. Planes and hot-air balloons carry special ads, while trucks, vans, and scooters advertise on-the-go businesses like radio news and emergency medical services. Local landmarks and historical sites are also depicted.

At first, Eddy and Beckman were involved primarily in ad sales. They contracted their printing out, and hired local artists to draw up the maps. Today, they're more focused on training and licensing. There are more than sixty-eight Fiesta licensees marketing cartoon maps nationwide. Eddy and Beckman offer their licensees training, sample maps and business cards, access to Fiesta's experienced art department, and ongoing counseling and advice.

The partners report that the business is both simple and profitable. "Everybody who's in business is looking for new ways of advertising," Eddy says. Providing a low-cost alternative to some of the more expensive traditional advertising vehicles has helped put Fiesta on the map.

|IT'S A HIT!

> Bill Shane left a job as bank president to make tapes of fantasy sports broadcasts. "My career was in finance," he says, "but my dreams were in sports."

Sportcasters will tell you they've given up a lot for their careers. Huntington Beach, California, business owner Bill Shane is no different. When he started SportsDreams, Inc. in 1988, he left a job as president of a bank. Why? "I wanted to be entrepreneurial," he says. "And besides, it's so much fun!"

What's all the fun about? Sports, believe it or not. Shane makes personalized broadcasts of world-class sporting events with his clients as the stars. The tapes come complete with crowd noises, sound effects, and various personal touches (in one he identifies the star's training diet as "burned hash browns;" in another he cries, "You're blind, ump!" in Japanese). All told, Shane offers thirty-five different scripts, which he tailors to each client. In Shane's world, nine-year-olds win the World Karate Championship and grandmothers beat out Flo-Jo in the 100 meters. It's a stretch, he admits, but one clients are willing to pay for.

Making the leap from banking executive to home sportscaster may sound intimidating, but Shane takes it in his stride. To him, the new business was practically fated. "I've been doing this for fun for about six years for friends and relatives," he explains. "I heard about someone doing something similar on the East Coast and thought I'd give it a try. I always wanted to have my own business, and I thought this idea was a good one."

He invested only $7,000 in the new business. With that, he bought two tape decks, mixing equipment, headphones, a microphone, and enough professional studio time to record a library of sound effects. A toy company agreed to feature his tapes in their Christmas catalog—that was his first advertising. Since then, he's realized that kids aren't his target market. "About 83 percent are adults," he says. "And most of the recipients are men." He now advertises in the classified sections of business, regional, and upscale publications around the country. In his first year, he sold about four hundred tapes.

The sportscasts aren't cheap—prices start at $100—but then neither is production. Shane interviews clients personally to get the dirt on the proposed "hero." He takes down favorite expressions, favorite foods, hair color, pet peeves—in all, some fifty items—and weaves them into the story line. Writing the script takes a good hour and recording in Shane's basement studio takes even longer. Luckily, it's all in fun. "I like the creativity of it," he says. "People love it. About 40 percent of my customers write to me and say, 'You should have seen the look on his face. . . .'"

In the future, Shane envisions a larger company with additional sportscasters and maybe a few new products (after this idea, we can hardly wait to see what's next). Meanwhile, he's enjoying his new lifestyle. Trotting down to the basement to record grandpa's triumph over the Yankees may not be as glamorous as the world of high finance, but it's good enough for Shane. "I love the independence of it," he says, "not having to wear a suit—not even having to wear shoes. I can't get over it: People pay me for having fun."

5

CAREER AND FINANCIAL SERVICES

Résumé Writing Service

Business:

Writing, typing, and reproducing résumés

Basic Equipment and Expenses:

$10,000

Necessities:

Computer system for word processing, paper, telephone, typewriter, copier (can be leased)

Experience Required:

Must have a thorough knowledge of local business and industry, writing skills and marketing know-how also critical

Inside Tip:

Shop around for the best word-processing system. Because frequent copy changes are routine, the efficiency of your word processing can play a major role in your success.

Job seekers place tremendous value on their résumés— and with good reason. Until they meet with prospective employers in person, a résumé is all they have to sell their skills. Presentation is all. Yet it's hard to know what to include and how to convey it. For many job seekers, typing alone presents a dilemma.

Enter the résumé writing service. Whether the job requires simple typing or complete writing and composition services, a good résumé writing firm can make the most of any résumé. And in the process, they take a tremendous strain off what is usually an anxiety-ridden time.

Barbara Maxwell, a Tulsa, Oklahoma, résumé and job-search consultant, reports that this business is more than just typing. "We have a client's career earnings at stake," says Maxwell. "To be good, you have to have a tremendous community awareness. You have to know how to express the intangible, and you have to understand different businesses well enough to present different people in the best possible light. I have to know enough about manufacturing, for instance, to write a welder's résumé. You've got to be able to write to a beat, because you have a limited amount of space to work with." And you have to sell. "It's salesmanship as much as anything else," says Maxwell. "It's selling people's skills on paper."

Maxwell's fees range from $22.50 for typing and reproduction to about $165 for a complete portfolio. Most of her clients are upwardly mobile professionals: attorneys, accountants, technical personnel, managers, and graduating students. Maxwell stresses that most of her clients are not in dire straits. "They know how to help themselves, they just need a little direction," she explains. "Once they get on the right track, they take the ball and run with it." Most clients, she reports, are capable of writing their own résumés, but realize that they can get better results faster by working with a professional. "I have nine years of experience in job searching," Maxwell says. "I hope none of my clients can match that."

While many résumé-writing services provide just that— simple writing and typing—Maxwell feels that providing some additional expertise is important. "We help people create job-search strategies," she explains. To that end, she can provide clients with tips on conducting a job search. She even publishes a directory of local industries.

Maxwell also emphasizes that keeping clients in a positive frame of mind is a large part of her job. "I will never ask a client why they are being terminated from a job," she says. "I will never talk about the past—only the future. We focus on what a person can do. I will never tell an untruth on a résumé, but I think there's no reason to say what a client can't do. People are coming in at a very traumatic time in their lives. We're selling a positive attitude as much as anything."

In addition to working with individual clients, Maxwell does corporate outplacement, helping departing employees gear up for job hunting. If she had it to do over again, she says she would put more energy into this area and less into individual clients. Not only does corporate outplacement represent a lucrative market, but it's also a more predictable way of doing business. "When you've got an office full of people and a big corporate account comes in, it can really get— exciting," Maxwell jokes.

FINANCIAL PLANNING

Business:

Helping clients reach their financial goals through savings, budgeting, investment, and management

Basic Equipment and Expenses:

$5,000

Necessities:

Basic office equipment (typewriter, calculator), telephone, personal computer highly recommended

Experience Required:

No set standards for licensing, most financial planners come from backgrounds in insurance, accounting, financial services, and the law

Inside Tip:

To establish immediate credibility, training and/or certification are recommended. Home study is available through organizations like the College for Financial Planning in Denver.

With so many options available to investors these days, the need for qualified financial consultants continues to increase. Individuals with solid backgrounds in finance, accounting, or risk management—or anyone willing to learn these fields through course study—are prime candidates for the growing field of financial planning.

What does a financial planner do? Basically speaking, he or she oversees a client's finances. Typical duties might include calculating a client's net worth, analyzing cash flow, devising a workable budget, and formulating written plans for accumulating assets. He or she should also be familiar with tax laws, investments, and insurance. Since most financial planners specialize in a single area—say risk management or investments—they may call in experts in other fields to fill in any gaps of knowledge. Still, a working knowledge of all aspects of financial planning is essential to doing a good job.

Currently, there are 150,000 financial planners in the United States, up from just a handful twenty years ago. High earning potential makes this an attractive field. Planners charge hourly fees of $80 to $175, or bring in lucrative commissions.

Technically, you don't need any training or certification to become a financial planner. However, to establish credibility in the field, it's best to have some related experience and/or a designation as a Certified Financial Planner (CFP) or Chartered Financial Consultant (ChFC). "We're dealing with people's money," says Northbrook, Illinois, financial planner Ben Baldwin, president of Baldwin Financial Systems, Inc. "It's important to us that we really know what we're doing. Education is the key factor in building and maintaining a successful practice." Investigate colleges in your area or home study courses for more information on education in this field.

For More Information:

American Society of Chartered Life Underwriters
& Chartered Financial Consultants
270 Bryn Mawr Avenue
Bryn Mawr, Pennsylvania 19010
(215) 526-2500

College for Financial Planning
4965 South Monaco Street
Denver, Colorado 80237
(303) 220-1200

International Association for Financial Planning
Two Concourse Parkway, Suite 800
Atlanta, Georgia 30328
(404) 395-1605

National Association of Personal Financial Advisors
3726 Olentangy River Road
Columbus, Ohio 43214
(614) 457-8200

American Association of Personal Financial Planners
21031 Ventura Blvd., Suite 903
Woodland Hills, California 91364
(818) 348-5400

TAX PREPARATION SERVICE

Business:

Preparing tax returns and providing year-round advice on tax planning

Basic Equipment and Expenses:

$6,000

Necessities:

Telephone, home computer, adding machine, pencils, pens, tax manuals, tax forms, copy machine (it's possible to lease one)

Experience Required:

Familiarity with tax laws essential; bookkeeping/accounting experience extremely desirable; business sense a plus

Inside Tip:

Building a year-round clientele can take time. If your job permits, start the business on a seasonal basis first. By the second tax season, repeat business and referrals should up your volume.

   If finance is your forte, consider starting a tax-preparation service. Despite the IRS's best efforts to simplify forms, there continue to be millions of Americans who will pay almost any price to have their taxes done.

Lack of time is only one reason people seek tax services. Ignorance and simple aversion, says Fort Worth, Texas, accountant Sarah Parsons, are more commonly cited. Parsons owns Records Unlimited, a tax preparation and accounting service that caters to both individuals and businesses. Since she started the business in 1976, Parsons has seen all kinds of clients—including a foreign student who thought his W-2 form was provided for his information only. By the time he contacted Parsons, he had neglected to submit three years' worth of forms.

While most Americans are savvier than that, many still need help with their annual returns. Learning the nuances of America's tax laws can be taxing at best—not to mention the ongoing task of keeping up with legislative changes. Moreover, mistakes can be costly, considering the various penalties and interest charges that apply. Individuals aren't alone in their confusion, either. Many businesses— especially small companies that can't afford full-time accounting departments—need the services of a qualified tax service.

To start, you need the basic tools of the trade: an adding machine, some pencils and pens, tax manuals and forms, and a telephone. Having a copier on hand is important, unless you don't mind frequent trips to the nearest copy shop. If you're short on start-up funds, consider buying a used copier or leasing one until you can afford to buy.

Parsons strongly recommends getting a home computer with accounting software as well. "Nowadays, if you're not computer-wise, you're wasting your time," Parsons says. "You can't compete in the business world without computer literacy. Three of us [in Parson's firm] do the work that five or six people would manually." Just the basics are enough, according to Parsons. "Don't go to school to learn about computers—they'll teach you how the car works instead of showing you how to drive," she warns. "Find someone to teach you what you need to know."

Parsons learned much of the business in school: first in college, then through continuing education courses. But she stresses that simple accounting skills are not enough to maintain a regular clientele. "You have to be the kind of person people can trust," says Parsons, "as much as being knowledgeable." Parsons really takes the time to serve her clients. She tutored one business owner on his home computer as a favor. When another client moved from Dallas to Atlanta, he refused to switch to another accountant. In addition to tax preparation, Parsons provides payroll processing and bookkeeping services, as well as a lot of friendly business advice. "You can't do this without doing some counseling," she says.

To those considering a tax preparation service, Parsons offers these words of caution: "When you start out, you starve," she says. "It takes five or six years to build your business, and you have to be good."

CLAIMS TO FAME

Millions of Americans never bother to file their health insurance claims, others simply don't know how. In 1984, Joan and Richard Kirkpatrick set out to change all that.

In 1985, Joan Kirkpatrick's mother suffered a massive stroke. Along with the emotional turmoil that accompanied the illness came a deluge of bills to pay and forms to fill out. "I had her other affairs to deal with," Kirkpatrick recalls. "I had children and a full-time job and a home to take care of. I certainly wasn't in the mood to delve into paperwork."

Thus, Kirkpatrick experienced firsthand the need for medical claims processing services. And Kirkpatrick's husband Richard got plenty of practice processing forms— though by that time he was already a pro.

Richard Kirkpatrick founded Med-I-Claims Services, Inc. in 1984, after dealing with a pile of medical claims at his former accounting job. He asked, "What in the world do people do if they haven't worked with detailed paperwork before?" "Or what if they haven't done it in years?" says Joan. The answer, of course, is that they don't file their claims. Or they file them incorrectly and aren't able to collect their benefits. It seemed a terrible waste to Richard, who decided to make it his business to file claims properly for his clients.

With a nominal investment, Richard launched the firm from a basement office, but soon moved quarters to commercial space. "As the clientele grew, it became worrisome for us to run the business from home," Joan explains. "The house has a terraced front, so when clients came over, they had to climb two flights of steps. Then, they had to walk down to the basement." Moving to a separate office wasn't the only concession to growth. Shortly after the business started, Joan retired from her job at a local bank to pitch in.

The business proved not only profitable, but newsworthy. In 1987, a local television station ran a story on Med-I-Claims on the news. That feature led to national coverage on *Good Morning America* and CNN. "We started getting phone calls," Joan says, "from all over the country. The first call I got, I was blown away. Just being on the local news was more than we had hoped for. The phone calls continued for months, and we realized we had to do something for all these people who wanted more information."

Sadly, the Kirkpatricks had another reason for recording the workings of their business in writing. Richard's health began to falter and they worried that he might become too ill to run the company. Their son-in-law, Rick Yates, helped them produce a manual on medical claims processing, which they now sell to aspiring processors. In the summer of 1988, Richard died of cancer.

Though she describes the loss as "devastating," Joan is putting renewed effort into building the business. In addition to selling the manuals, Med-I-Claims also is planning to conduct seminars in future months. Joan feels strongly about the services her company provides. "We like to treat each client as an individual," she says. "I think they deserve that. If they've been through an illness, they're frustrated enough by their ill-health—they don't need problems.

"We're very unique in that we do not sell insurance," Joan continues. "We're able to act as an advocate for our clients. We believe that people who pay for their insurance deserve their benefits. But if nothing is filed, no money is going to be paid."

6

ON THE ROAD

MOBILE LOCKSMITH SERVICE

Business:

Providing the services of a lock shop, but on wheels. Lock-outs, repairs, and installations comprise most of the business

Basic Equipment and Expenses:

$10,000

Necessities:

Telephone, transportation (van or truck preferred), basic locksmithing equipment including code machine, code books, duplicating machine, blank keys, etc.

Experience Required:

Must be a trained locksmith. Instruction is available through correspondence courses and vocational schools

Inside Tip:

Look for areas of expansion or special expertise. Safe work or commercial sales are just a few areas to explore.

Honolulu, Hawaii entrepreneur Al Martin gave up two lock shops to focus on his mobile service. "In a shop, you can only cover so much area," he explains. "I opened a second shop, but there wasn't enough business for two. It's so expensive to maintain a location, it just wasn't worth it." So Martin converted his VW Diesel Rabbit into a lockmobile and became a roving lock doctor. Today—several years and a new van later—he reports, "I enjoy the mobile business 100 percent more than I did my shops."

To become a mobile locksmith, you'll need training. Martin learned the business by taking a correspondence course and apprenticing with a local locksmith. "I was retired from the service, so I wasn't that concerned with income," he recalls. "I told this locksmith that I'd work for him for nothing to learn the business while I was taking the course. He hired me on the spot." Soon after that—in 1973—Martin ventured out on his own, and he's been in the locksmithing business ever since.

Aside from being qualified, dependable, and honest, Martin believes the secret to success in mobile locksmithing is location. While a retail location is extraneous, locating your business in a well-populated, affluent community will help. "You have to be where the people are," he warns. "If you're not in a good area, you'll be sitting by the phone waiting for a call." Another consideration is that most mobile locksmiths are on call twenty-four-hours a day. Be prepared to work odd hours, or to find an employee to cover some shifts.

Martin reports some colorful experiences in his travels, including going from party to party fixing locks one New Year's Eve, and discovering that the locked-out car he was working on belonged to a large, irate man who knew nothing about Martin's services. "It's a good business," he says. "You get to meet many, many interesting people."

RESTAURANT DELIVERY SERVICE

Business:

Delivering food from the restaurant to the customers' doorsteps

Basic Equipment and Expenses:

$10,000

Necessities:

Transportation, telephone, Styrofoam chest(s) for carrying food, brochures/flyers

Experience Required:

None

Inside Tip:

Nail down a workable communications system before you get started. Who will receive customer calls? Who will do the driving? How will the two communicate with one another?

Pizza again? For millions of Americans who haven't the will to go out and buy their daily bread, pizza delivery is their sole alternative. But what if they could have filet mignon instead? Or tandoori chicken? Or enchiladas rancheras? A growing number of restaurants are responding to the demand for delivery by offering their own door-to-door service. But many can't afford the extra manpower—or they don't want to be bothered.

Enter the restaurant delivery service. Armed with a reliable car, a Styrofoam chest, and a solid knowledge of your local area, you can provide the deliveries that restaurants don't. Working professionals in search of an easy dinner at home are a prime market, as are overtimers, and the corporate lunch crowd.

John Pugsley's company, Restaurant Express, has been providing restaurant delivery services to the Newport Beach, California, area since 1987. Pugsley originally conceived of the idea as a venture for his out-of-work daughter. "I had gotten some take-out [from my favorite restaurant] a few months earlier and I thought, 'Boy, it would be nice if somebody would deliver from that restaurant to the home,'" he says. When he calculated how much might be made by offering just that service, he decided to launch the business himself.

For a four dollar delivery fee, Restaurant Express will whisk a meal from any of over forty participating restaurants to the customer's door. In addition to the fee, Restaurant Express makes money on commissions from the participating eateries. In its first year of business, Restaurant Express served between 60,000 and 70,000 meals. In 1988, Pugsley estimates making about 2,000 deliveries—or $30,000 in gross revenues—weekly. Plans for the future include going public and possibly franchising.

With volume like that, Pugsley clearly isn't a small-time operator. But with a little ingenuity you might be able to follow in his footsteps. The trick, according to Pugsley, is developing a system. "We've finally come up with a very, very effective formula," he says. In the future, he looks forward to becoming "the Federal Express of the restaurant business."

MESSENGER/DELIVERY SERVICE

Business:

Delivering documents, airline tickets, gifts, etc., from one door to another

Basic Equipment and Expenses:

$5,000

Necessities:

Transportation, telephone, maps, order forms

Experience Required:

Ability to navigate city streets (even the obscure ones), marketing and organizational skills

Inside Tip:

Take on additional people as contractors to save on paperwork and liability. As payment, Grace Bartlett splits all delivery fees with her runners—which gives them an added incentive to do an efficient job.

In this book, we highlight all kinds of mobile businesses: mobile locksmithing, mobile food delivery, mobile pet grooming. But here, let us be purists. You can create a profitable business simply by being mobile.

Take a cue from Phoenix, Arizona, entrepreneur Grace Bartlett. Her company, Graceful Deliveries, transports anything from legal documents to live lobsters for a typical cost of $16.80, depending on distance. Since Bartlett started the company in 1985, it's expanded to include four full-time drivers, four part-time drivers, and a new partner, Beverly Tyson. Graceful Deliveries services 275 regular accounts and, in 1988, billed $140,000.

Not bad for a business Bartlett originally intended to run part-time. Working alone with her car, some order forms, and a telephone, Bartlett began with a single account: a friend's travel agency. "She needed someone to run [airline] tickets," she says. Bartlett "didn't like working for other people," so she quit her job as a data-entry supervisor and hit the open road. Running a delivery service alone wasn't easy. But, says Bartlett, "obviously, I was fast enough to handle it."

The market for delivery services is diverse. Corporations use messengers to deliver time-sensitive documents and run outside errands. Some florists and specialty-gift companies contract their deliveries out to independent services. Restaurants are another potential source of business. Then, there are the odd jobs. On Secretaries' Day, Graceful Deliveries presented some 150 bouquets of roses in a three-hour time span.

"You have to be a jack-of-all-trades and know how to do everything in this business," says Bartlett. "You can go for two years and never draw a salary, just putting money back into the business. You need organization and the will to make it. When people told me it couldn't be done, I knew I had to do it."

LUNCH DELIVERY SERVICE

Business:

Preparing lunch items and delivering them to offices and other workplaces

Basic Equipment and Expenses:

$10,000

Necessities:

Health-licensed kitchen, cooking equipment (stove, pots, knives, bowls, etc.), transportation, portable cooler on wheels, telephone

Experience Required:

Cooking and marketing are the primary skills. Having cooked in a commercial environment is a big plus

Inside Tip:

To secure a health-licensed kitchen on a shoestring, consider sharing quarters with a restaurant or catering company. Churches, community centers, and schools are other potential sources of rentable space.

Shelia Young, owner of Young's Secretarial Service in Oakland, California, swears she hasn't had lunch out in four years. Young isn't alone. Increasingly, office employees are eating in to get a head start on the afternoon's work—or to take a bite out of overtime hours. Yet packing a lunch can be a hassle, especially when leisure hours are at a premium.

Lunch delivery services bridge the gap between dining out and bringing a bag. Typical delivery items include pasta salad, sandwiches, and microwaveable lasagne. Prices are generally modest—considerably lower than a restaurant meal. And consumers aren't the only ones who save. Start-up costs for a lunch-delivery service are substantially lower than for a restaurant—a boon for food-minded entrepreneurs who don't have a lot to spend.

Billy Koskoff and former partner Jerry Singer launched Los Angeles-based L.A. Daily from the back of Singer's parents' house. Koskoff's initial investment: "I think I put up a couple hundred dollars." Though Koskoff (and most local health departments) doesn't recommend starting a lunch-delivery business from a home kitchen, he does observe that it got his company off to a winning start. L.A. Daily currently delivers lunch to businesses all around the L.A. basin via a network of about fifty independent delivery people. On an average day, it sells three thousand sandwiches, salads, and entrées.

Koskoff is a former caterer whose business, The Moveable Feast, provided eats to some of the poshest L.A. events. Successful as he was, Koskoff welcomed the opportunity to do something less demanding. "Catering was a killer business," he says. "I was working seven days a week, doing thirty parties a week. I have four kids, and I like to see them."

According to Koskoff, good lunch delivery is in demand. In Los Angeles, he says, the competition is getting stiff. But the service certainly isn't losing popularity. "It's a service that most people want. People will write letters asking us to come by." If building management puts up a fuss about solicitors in their hallways, customers rally in the service's favor. "They'll order food in advance so we have a reason to go into the building," he says. In fact, most building managers view L.A. Daily as an asset to their building—just one more service they can offer without charge.

Koskoff emphasizes the creative challenge involved in doing his job well. "We have to keep the clients interested," he explains. "That means menu changes. It's not like a restaurant where they come to you. A hot item can turn very lukewarm if people get tired of it. You have to keep offering something new." Koskoff tests the popularity of new items by running them as weekly specials first. He changes the menus wholesale once or twice a year to keep things fresh. Working within a budget keeps Koskoff on his toes creatively. "I can't go out and buy prosciutto or grouse," he says. "People only want to spend three or four dollars on lunch. I have to be practical." Still, he maintains a high level of quality and innovation: His turkey-and-smoked-gouda sandwiches and Caesar salads are definitely a cut above the usual fast food.

Koskoff credits his success to a combination of good luck and a timely concept. "A good idea goes a long way," he says. "If you've got something people want, you're in business."

IF FOOD COULD DRIVE

> Jean Triner's working friends longed for her home-cooked meals. Now they can buy them on a moment's notice.

There are a hundred reasons not to cook dinner tonight. You're working late. You're too tired. You broke your leg in seven places. You just moved in and the refrigerator is empty. You have a new baby. You don't know a scallop from a shallot. Then again, maybe you just don't want to.

Use any excuse you like: Jean Triner understands. Triner is founder of Moment's Notice Cuisine in Cleveland, a service that delivers gourmet meals to customers who can store them in the freezer or devour them on the spot. Whether you're in the mood for vegetarian lasagne or prime rib of beef, Moment's Notice probably has something that will hit the spot—and you don't have to cruise the supermarket aisles or don an apron to enjoy it.

Before she launched Moment's Notice in 1988, Triner was a human resources manager for a national corporation. Despite the demands of dual careers, Triner and her husband always took the time to have a good meal after work. "It was a way to unwind," Triner says. Triner's meals were the envy of her working friends, who were tired of cold pizza and take-out Chinese. Why couldn't they have home-cooked meals delivered to their homes?

Why indeed? Triner didn't do the obvious. She didn't heat up her own oven and get to work. Instead, she took classes on business planning. She tested recipes. She tried menus out on friends. She studied pricing, marketing, finance. And she networked, the result of which is a list of part-time professional suppliers who provide her with everything from salad to pie. All told, Triner spent a year getting her business together. But because of her exhaustive planning, she was able to start out from home with no kitchen (suppliers have their own facilities), no professional equipment, and no storefront.

"Starting out with a small investment worked out well for me," Triner says. "If you can find out whether or not you like a business before you put a lot of money into it, it's really ideal."

So far, Triner likes it. "There are many satisfactions in this business," she says. "One of them is helping my suppliers—I call them mini-entrepreneurs—get their start. One of my suppliers started out wanting to open a pie shop. Now, she still wants to do that, but maybe in a few years." Triner's customers are equally grateful. "There's such a need out there," she reports. "I have so many stories about the people who use my services. There are so many different reasons they call."

From the beginning, marketing has been no problem for Triner. The local paper did a story on her before she even opened the business, and the free publicity has continued ever since. Triner has appeared on television talk shows, on radio broadcasts, and in *The Wall Street Journal.* Between the publicity and word of mouth, she often has more interest then she can handle. She is comfortable with the thirty to forty orders she averages each week (the average order is fifty to sixty dollars). But special requests can be overwhelming.

"One of the biggest challenges has been narrowing the focus of the business," Triner says. "In the beginning, I was so eager, I'd say 'yes' to everything—like providing food for a party of two hundred. You can't be all things to all people. I have to remember that.

"Right now, my business is focused on the east side [of Cleveland], but I've had a lot of interest from the west side," she continues. "I'm thinking about that now. I've also had some downtown offices call. A lot of lawyers down there work nights and they're sick of the usual take-out. That's another idea I'm considering. But I want to keep the growth manageable. Last summer the summer came and went before I realized there was a summer. I've made a commitment to myself and my husband that that's not going to happen this year."

Triner has been able to delegate two large responsibilities: food preparation and delivery. Though she's constantly testing new recipes (especially low-cholesterol and low-calorie dishes), the food she sells comes from suppliers. Triner also has two regular part-time delivery people who handle the bulk of the driving. "I like to do the deliveries myself the first time someone orders, just to establish rapport," she says. She also handles the finances, administration, marketing, and a vigorous program of customer service. "People are great about giving you feedback," she says.

Triner doesn't miss the corporate lifestyle much these

days. Having the freedom to make her own decisions—without the approval of supervisors and committees—is the greatest reward. "You have the agony and the ecstasy," she says, "because if you make a mistake, there's no one else to blame. But the effort you put in is commensurate with the results. In a corporation, the connection isn't that immediate." She enjoys working from home because she can "work in some nonbusiness things when there's a spare moment." On the other hand, "It's facing me twenty-four-hours a day, and there's always more work to do."

The advice Triner offers is twofold: prepare yourself well and run your business on your own terms. "Do your homework first," she says. "Utilize the resources that are available to you. Try to find a small business organization like COSE [the Council Of Smaller Enterprises] or SCORE [Service Core Of Retired Executives] and plug into them."

Also, consider the quality of your life in your business decisions. "I think there's a new strain of entrepreneurs that have been successful in other careers and have gone into business to find something different," Triner says. "We're trying to take some of the strain and pain out of growing a business. So many people will tell you that you have to give 180 percent to a business. And for the first year, that's been true. But it's also important to find some balance in life, to keep your business at a level that makes you happy."

7

GET YOUR PROMOTION

SPECIALTY ADVERTISING BROKERAGE

Business:

Matching company with specialty items that will effectively promote their businesses. Some examples: imprinted pens, personalized T-shirts, awards, gifts, incentives

Basic Equipment and Expenses:

$7,500

Necessities:

Telephone, business cards, samples of various specialty products

Experience Required:

Knowledge of existing products extremely helpful

Inside Tip:

Research. Before you devote your life to this field, buy some specialty advertising items for your new company to get a feel for the business.

San Francisco bridal consultant Janet Ellinwood says the best advertising she's ever done was on a pen. "I have some felt-tip pens with rainbow caps that have my business name and phone number on them," she explains. "I get more calls from those, because people keep them and remember my service."

According to the Specialty Advertising Association International (SAAI) in Dallas, Texas, American companies spend over $23 billion on incentives and premiums every year. And these go far beyond your usual pens and T-shirts. "This market includes everything from imprinted jalapeño suckers to Rolex watches," says Glen Holt, president of Certified Marketing Consultants in Scottsdale, Arizona. "We've done anything from spatulas to ice scrapers."

Holt's company helps manufacturers link up with specialty advertising brokers. Over the years, he's seen many changes in the industry. "The good news in this business is that an entrepreneur can enter the industry for a relatively low cost," Holt says. "The bad news is that we attracted a lot of opportunists as a result." Since the seventies, the SAAI has been raising standards for specialty ad brokers. Consequently, "The professional level of our industry has risen substantially in the past decade or so," according to Holt. Today, specialty advertising firms rely on good management, not fast-talking sales tactics, to endure.

What does a specialty advertising broker do? According to Carl Badgett of Grotte Advertising in Houston, the job is to design a unique program to meet a client's promotional needs—whatever those needs may be. Promotional items (like Ellinwood's rainbow pens), employee awards, and client gifts are just a few of the requests clients have. A specialty ad firm does not stock items in mass quantities: Simply having a selection of samples is enough, making inventory requirements fairly modest. Badgett stresses, however, that samples alone don't make a business.

Coming up with suggestions that are both inventive and appropriate is Badgett's most challenging task. After sixteen years in the business, Badgett is well-versed in what's available from manufacturers. For newcomers, he warns, that knowledge could take years to acquire. "You have to learn who has what," he says. "It was quite a different market when I started. Since then, everybody's getting into the specialty business," including makers of leather and china, to name a few. "The best thing to do to learn the business is work internally," he suggests. "It takes time and there's no way around that."

Yet Holt reports that the business is well worth learning. "Even in recession years, where all areas of advertising were hurt, ad specialties continued to grow—not quickly, but still," he says. "Large corporations find that they can spend millions on television ads, and people still don't remember them. The strength of this industry is that corporate America loves specialties. They work."

SALE COORDINATOR

Business:

Staging and promoting garage sales, yard sales, moving sales, estate sales, etc.

Basic Equipment and Expenses:

$5,000

Necessities:

Telephone, transportation, tags, wrapping materials, cash box. The following equipment may be purchased used: tables, table covers, jewelry cases, garment racks, cabinets

Experience Required:

Avowed garage-sale addicts are at an advantage. Sales, promotional, and organizational skills are necessary

Inside Tip:

Marketing this business can be tricky. (If there's been a death in the family, you won't want to knock on the family's door with a flyer in hand.) Start by contacting real-estate offices and even lawyers to get referrals.

Several years ago, Fair Lawn, New Jersey, entrepreneur Beverly Michael taught a class on running a garage sale for a local adult-education program. "I was surprised at how many people didn't know the basics of putting on a sale," says Michael. She was also surprised when some of her former students called to ask for her help in staging their own events. It wasn't long before Michael realized there was a business in this, and Bev Michael Promotion was born.

Michael helps families sell their unwanted furniture, clothing, accessories, and knickknacks through what are commonly called tag sales, moving sales, or estate sales. Make no mistake: Michael doesn't do run-of-the-mill garage sales. People who have a few lamps and a pair of broken skis to get rid of can hawk their own wares. Michael's clients have at least three rooms full of furniture to sell.

Most clients contact her because they're moving. "Moving is so costly," says Michael, "that people have become selective about what they want to move. Sometimes they decide they want to make a clean sweep and buy all new furniture. Other times, they have grown children who aren't living with them anymore, and they have extra bedroom sets they don't need." Families also contact Michael when a family member has died, and they are selling the house. Michael takes the otherwise painful task of clearing a home for sale off the grieving family's hands.

What Michael brings to a tag sale is more than convenience, however. She also provides a professional touch.

First, she has a raft of fixtures and accessories, including garment racks, display cases, and coordinated table covers. "When I'm set up," she says, "it's as if you've walked into a Kmart." She offers shoppers advice on getting the nicks out of worn wood furniture and the stains out of the upholstery. If the sale is large, she calls on friends and family to help. When the sale is over, she makes sure the remnants are donated to charity and the house is cleaned. "I know how to price things. I know how to sell things. And I know how to expedite them," she says.

Michael works strictly on commission. In New Jersey, the business is seasonal, so her volume varies from month to month. When business is brisk, she brings in a tidy profit; when times are slower, she enjoys spending time with her children. She points out that aggressive marketing isn't really appropriate in this business—good news for your ad budget, but sometimes limiting when business needs a boost. Aside from occasional ads in the local paper, most of her business comes by referral.

Michael urges only the most avid tag-sale fans to get into the business. "People think it's easy because they see me selling things and they think, 'All she has to do is sit there and collect the money,'" Michael laments. "That's not true. You have to lug things around. You have to know how to price things, and how to sell." At times, she's had to defuse tensions between owners and shoppers. "It's terribly emotional for them to watch a home taken apart," she says. "I usually tell them to take the day off."

For avowed addicts, though, this business can be both fun and rewarding. Michael's own home furnishings come and go on a kind of revolving basis. "I'm constantly upgrading," she says. There's also enjoyment in chipping away at today's throwaway mentality. "Recycling is a sign of the times," Michael contends. "I've learned to take my kids to consignment shops as a result of this business. It's really a way of life."

INDEPENDENT AGENT

Business:

Promoting all varieties of talent—from local entertainment to writers and actors

Basic Equipment and Expenses:

$2,500

Necessities:

Telephone, typewriter, letterhead, advertising

Experience Required:

Should have thorough knowledge of the field you hope to promote; sales and marketing skills also essential

Inside Tip:

Says musical agent Nancy Carlin, "Find a particular subset of the business that you know a lot about." To become a musical agent, Carlin recommends working in the concert business, the recording industry—even in a record shop. Your expertise will really make a difference.

That talent and salesmanship don't mix seems to be one of the undeniable laws of nature. Artists, musicians, writers, and actors have complained for centuries that their talents go unnoticed (and uncompensated).

If you have sales ability and an appreciation for good talent, you can put these skills to work as an independent agent. You don't have to attract the likes of supermodels or superstars to be successful doing it, either. While representing actors, models, rock stars, and best-selling writers is very much a legitimate opportunity, it's also difficult to break into without inside knowledge of the business. On the other hand, promoting local and lesser-known talent is relatively accessible.

You will need some background before you begin. Nancy Carlin of Nancy Carlin Productions in Concord, California, started her career as a Renaissance musician. "I worked for the Renaissance Faire [a local festival of Renaissance arts and crafts] for a number of years," she says. "I met a lot of people there who were musicians and didn't have enough work." Carlin used her flair for marketing to land work for other musicians, and saw she had a genuine knack for promotion. One thing led to another, and Carlin ended up becoming an agent.

"I started out with my home phone and my own bank account," she says. "I spent virtually nothing. I can remember the days when buying a $150 ad was a big expense." Now, Carlin is a seasoned promoter. She books bands and musical groups for weddings, parties, festivals, fund-raisers, and winery events. She also books national tours for about ten different musical groups. All told, she brought in $600,000 in gross sales in 1988—not a bad haul for someone who "learned the business sliding by the seat of her pants."

Since sales is the essence of this business, you must be a first-rate marketer to succeed. Carlin, for instance, brings both energy and resourcefulness to her work. In a recent classified ad, under the heading "Weddings and Parties," Carlin advertised a list of wedding locations. She sent out the compiled list to everyone who inquired, along with information on her services. Not only did she snag her target market, but she also got a jump on her competition by reaching couples early in the planning process.

To yield the kind of sales she gets, Carlin represents about 150 acts and employs two assistants. They work out of an office attached to Carlin's home. It's good, she reports, because the commute is short. Then again, "The phone rings day and night. Desperate band members call me at 3 A.M."

Still, Carlin is making her living in a business she loves. Her newest venture is producing her own series of Scottish music concerts. The first year out, she broke even. This year, she plans to expand the focus and bring in more money. "The best thing is, I never get bored," she says. "I'm always listening to new music."

SEMINAR PROMOTION

Business:

Teaching and/or marketing instructional seminars

Basic Equipment and Expenses:

$7,500

Necessities:

Telephone, lesson plan, marketing agenda

Experience Required:

If you're planning to teach, you must have some area of expertise. This can range from antique quilt restoration to telemarketing techniques. On the sales end, you also must be able to reach and sell to your target market

Inside Tip:

Start small by teaching at a local night school or community college. You'll polish your teaching techniques and make potential contacts for future classes.

Americans are going back to school in record numbers— but not necessarily to traditional classrooms. At work, changing job responsibilities make continuing education a must. Experts estimate that American workers need training or retraining every two to five years. *Training* magazine estimates that American companies spend upwards of $32 billion annually on training. And work isn't all. Consumer workshops are also gaining in popularity as outlets for fast, fun knowledge and for meeting new people. Witness the popularity of Bill Zanker's Learning Annex: The nationwide adult-education courses bring in over $1 million monthly.

Almost any topic can be made into a seminar, but the most lucrative market is probably business. What do businesspeople need to learn about? Sales strategies, management skills, desktop publishing—just about any particular skill you can name.

To be a successful seminar presenter, though, you have to have some savvy. "Seminars are sort of like golf and tennis," says Minneapolis, Minnesota-based seminar presenter Bob Pike. "Anyone can play, but if you're going to be good at it, there's a lot more to it than just hitting a ball." Pike has had a flair for public speaking since he won a statewide award in the eighth grade. After working as a pastor for a short time, he got involved in seminar sales. From there, he learned both the business and presentation ends of the business. In 1980, he decided to launch his own company, Resources for Organizations, Inc.

Pike paid his dues in the early days of his business. Once, he flew to Pittsburgh to find that only three people showed up for his seminar. Though he had a strong compulsion to cancel, Pike opted to go on with the class. "I decided that if I wasn't going to put my all into it for three people, I would never get seventy-five or a hundred people to attend," he says. And a good thing he did. Two of those three attendees turned out to have strong connections, and referred some $18,000 worth of business to him over the next several years.

Because of early ups and downs in the seminar business, Pike suggests starting out part-time. "Businesses take longer to start than we think, because entrepreneurs are optimists by nature," he says. "Put as little pressure on yourself as possible. People don't want to deal with desperate people; they want to deal with successful people." Pike started his own business out of his basement—a location that he sometimes pines for in his current, more corporate offices. He also advises substituting "sweat for dollars." Wherever possible, he's cut corners by doing menial tasks himself. "I had 10,000 pieces of mail on my living-room floor with my kids stuffing and sorting envelopes," he recalls. "It was fun for the family and it saved me $150."

Otherwise, the most important concern should be providing useful, accessible information. "Your success is going to be driven on your content," Pike says. "Ultimately, if you have practical information that people can put to work immediately, you should be well-received." In terms of building a business, Pike recommends constant contemplation. "Don't consider that once you finish a seminar that you say goodbye and that's it," he says. "Ask yourself what else you can offer these people that will help them in their ongoing development. Always look for the next step."

PRESS ON

Armed with a borrowed typewriter and a Rolodex, public-relations consultant Gary Pike launched a million-dollar business, bit by frugal bit.

When Gary Pike started his own public-relations firm in 1983, he had talent, confidence, and determination. On the other hand, he did not have an office, a staff, or a bulging bank account. Pike launched his San Francisco firm, Pike Communications, from his dining room with a borrowed typewriter and his trusty Rolodex. He had one account, a retailer in Berkeley, but he "didn't know how to bill them."

Today, Pike still calls accounting his worst weakness. But with nearly $1 million in billings, he doesn't have to handle it himself. From its offices in the heart of San Francisco's financial district, Pike Communications handles everything from media relations to promotional brochures, catalogs, and special events. The road from Pike's original home office hasn't been paved with gold. In fact, part of the secret to Pike's success is sheer frugality.

Of course, ability also played a major role. Before launching his own business, Pike handled public relations for various nonprofit and government agencies, including the California Coastal Commission and the National Park Service. He also handled in-house marketing and public relations for Victoria's Secret, the nationwide lingerie chain.

At twenty-eight, Pike wasn't thinking of starting a business: He liked his job. But when Victoria's Secret was sold, Pike and twenty-five other employees found themselves out of work. "I was devastated," Pike recalls. "All of a sudden, I didn't have a job anymore." He rode the ferries around the San Francisco Bay, did a little soul-searching, and realized that his predicament might be a blessing in disguise. "There was a lot of volatility and emotion and drama in the marketing departments I worked in," he says. "That's not me. I was looking for stability."

Suddenly, trying something new didn't seem like such a bad idea. When an outplacement counseling firm offered to help Pike polish his business skills in exchange for some marketing, he accepted. "I figured I had nothing to lose," he says.

Pike had little money to risk, so he made every dollar count. Instead of renting an office to start, he used his one-bedroom apartment for workspace. At first, he scheduled his meetings at his clients' offices. "My fear, of course, was that prospective clients wouldn't like dealing with someone who worked out of their home," he says. Soon, however, his clients started coming over for breakfast.

Office space wasn't the only area of savings. From the beginning, Pike has believed in used equipment. "If it works when you buy it, it's probably not going to break," he argues. To save a buck, he's attended bankruptcy auctions and shopped around for the cheapest phone-installation service. When the time came to rent commercial office space, he sublet portions of the office to other businesspeople until he needed them.

And if his business budget was streamlined, so were his personal finances. "You've got to set yourself up so that you need as little money as possible," he says, "so you can put every penny back into the business. I still don't take more money out of the business than I absolutely need. I'm thirty-four years old and I'm going to do this for another twenty years. I want this business to work, because I don't want to start another one."

Recently, Pike worried that leasing new, expanded offices in San Francisco's financial district would be biting off more than the business could chew. But a month after moving in, business had tripled. "I'm learning that the business really can grow," Pike says. "I've grown slowly, but I'm always sticking my neck out a little bit. I may lose a few nights' sleep [over my decisions], but my business always responds."

Pike is living proof that you don't need a lot of money to make a lot of money. While public relations has treated him well, he warns would-be publicists to get some experience before trying to follow in his footsteps. "Public relations isn't easy," he says, "it's a craft. It's a specialized skill. We really produce results—that's why we've been so successful.

"I never say 'no' to anyone," Pike continues. "If I don't know how to do something, by the time I hang up the phone, I know three people to call to find out how to do it."

8

THE FIX IS IN

POOL SERVICE

Business:

Cleaning and maintaining swimming pools

Basic Equipment and Expenses:

$3,000

Necessities:

Transportation, water treatment chemicals, pool-cleaning equipment

Experience Required:

Licensing required in some states, reliability is a high priority in maintaining good customer relations

Inside Tip:

As a sideline to your pool service, sell pool covers and accessories. Regular visits to clients' pools will give you the inside track.

Does working by the pool all day sound like your kind of business? Consider starting a pool service.

Count swimming-pool maintenance among the scores of chores around the house that working people don't want to handle themselves. Add to that market affluent people who simply don't do their own maintenance (time or no time), apartment and condominium complexes, hotels and motels, public swimming pools, and so on, and you'll get an idea of how extensive this market can be.

Pool cleaning involves both weekly maintenance (treating the water, cleaning the cement and tile) and opening and closing pools in the spring and winter. Some states require special licensing, especially to work on commercial accounts; some also have regulations on storing chemicals at home.

Pool services are well-suited to the home office. Because virtually all of your work takes place on the clients' premises, you don't need elaborate facilities or office equipment. And because of the seasonal nature of this business, working from home keeps overhead down during the winter months.

Bob Butler, owner of Butler's Pool Service in Vista, California, works out of his home. Though demand for his services in sunny California is ample, Butler keeps his accounts to about seventy. That way, he can work alone and "maintain a better, more personal relationship with customers.

"It's a great way to be on your own," he says.

HANDYMAN REFERRAL SERVICE

Business:

Matching clients with appropriate home-repair services, either from a single contractor or a variety of specialists

Basic Equipment and Expenses:

$2,500

Necessities:

Telephone, advertising, business cards

Experience Required:

None

Inside Tip:

Here's another option: Set yourself up as a directory. You can screen applicants to make sure they're reliable, then charge them a fee for being listed with your service.

Santa Clarita, California, entrepreneur Lee Loscalzo will tell you: A good handyman is hard to find. In 1988, Loscalzo got fed up waiting for her husband to do minor repairs around the house. "My husband is not a handyman," she confides. "But I could never find a reliable person to work on my house." Loscalzo solved that problem—and found herself a business to boot. She started Honey Do Kiss List, a service that matches homeowners with qualified repairpeople in a variety of fields.

"It cost me $35 for the initial ad in the paper," says Loscalzo. "I'm a licensed hairstylist: I figured I was gambling the cost of one haircut." It was a good gamble. In its first six months of business, Honey Do Kiss List grossed $40,000.

The business name is a bit of a patchwork. "Every woman has a 'honey do' list," says Loscalzo. "You know, 'Honey, do this,' and 'Honey, do that.' With my service, you can kiss those lists good-bye."

Indeed, Loscalzo's team can handle all kinds of tasks, from landscaping to sprinkler systems, from fixing drywall to assembling toys. Most of them are generalists—able to fix a squeaky door or a leaky faucet with equal aplomb. Others specialize in electronics or plumbing. They are all independent contractors.

The need for home-repair work is obvious. But why would consumers contact Loscalzo instead of hiring repairpeople themselves? For one thing, finding reliable help around the house isn't easy. Virtually every homeowner has had the experience of waiting for the plumber who never showed—or worse, the handyman who bore a shocking resemblance to Charles Manson. "When I did my market research," explains Loscalzo, "I found the two top considerations were visual [homeowners didn't want Manson lookalikes], and reliability. Every time they called someone, he wouldn't show up." Loscalzo guarantees the work. And her associates are all carefully screened for both skill and personality.

Another reason homeowners contact Loscalzo is she's visible. "I did a lot of advertising in the beginning in newspapers, through direct mail, on television, on the radio," she says. "The best thing I've found is a direct-mail coupon. Newspapers are also good." Loscalzo has developed contacts through a networking group she hosts. And she is also strong on follow-up, so she gets plenty of repeat business. "I keep on top of the men to make sure the work gets done," she says. "I have them check in with me when they get to a job. People are picky, picky, picky. I have to work hard to keep my customers happy."

INTERIOR PAINTING

Business:

Painting homes, apartments, offices, and commercial buildings

Basic Equipment and Expenses:

$2,500

Necessities:

Telephone, transportation, ladder, rollers with extension poles, brushes, paint

Experience Required:

General knowledge about paint helpful. Licensing may be required: Check your local government for details

Inside Tip:

Adding exterior painting and sandblasting services can increase your bottom line, but equipment costs may be prohibitive at first. Start out doing interiors and buy additional equipment for exteriors as your business grows.

Here's a skill most of us have, but few use professionally. Painting the interiors of homes, apartments, condominiums, and offices is a simple and inexpensive business to break into. New York City painter Michael Charley got started in 1988 with only $110 for some flyers and basic equipment. Though he admits he's "not making tons of money," he adds, "I've been very successful in proportion to the money I put in."

Most of Charley's clients are single professionals who don't have the time or energy to tackle a paint job alone. He charges about $100 a day plus materials for a basic paint job—lower rates, he says, than many of his competitors. "I hear that $24 an hour is typical around here," he says, "but companies that are larger and have a lot of overhead have to charge more." In addition to plain painting, Charley does special effects like sponge and marble finishes. "Those are the decorating trends right now," he explains, "and you make more money doing them."

Because he doesn't own a truck or van, Charley gets around primarily by subway. "It's not so great if you have to carry around a ladder," he says. But at many jobs, he's able to borrow ladders from building maintenance. The business is relatively easy, he reports. Probably the most difficult aspect of it is pricing. "There's a wild variation in price in this business," he says. "Then, a lot of buildings get their staff to paint the apartments, and that keeps the prices down."

Nonetheless, Charley enjoys the independence of being in business for himself. "When you have your own business, you get more respect, which is probably what I want the most," he says. "I wouldn't work for someone else, even if I were getting paid twice what I'm making now. I've become a strong believer in running your own business."

RADON DETECTION SERVICE

Business:

Marketing radon-detection kits to homeowners through any number of channels, including direct sales, retail distribution, and full-service testing

Basic Equipment and Expenses:

$2,500

Necessities:

Telephone, transportation, radon testing kits

Experience Required:

None if you send the kits off to a separate lab for examination

Inside Tip:

Check with your state and local governments to see if radon testing is required for new home sales in your area. If so, this is a good potential market for your services.

The U.S. Environmental Protection Agency recommends that every homeowner in the country test for the presence of radon. The Surgeon General warns that radon is dangerous, and can be hazardous to your health. What is radon and why are people so concerned about it?

Radon is a colorless, odorless gas that occurs naturally as a result of the breakdown of uranium in the earth's surface. During the past several years, the EPA has begun warning Americans that the radioactive gas, which is known to cause lung cancer, can accumulate in unhealthful levels in the home. By seeping in through cracks or drains in the foundations or basement of a house, radon can build up, especially during cold months when the house is otherwise sealed tight, and pose a health problem to residents.

Yet a relatively small percentage of homes have been tested for this deadly gas. According to Charles Quinlan of KSE Inc., a Sunderland, Massachusetts radon-testing lab, consumer interest in radon testing is growing. "Our sales are about 15 percent higher than they were a year ago," he says. "Following the Surgeon General's statement about the dangers of radon, we saw a heightened consumer interest. There was a spike in the business, then it calmed down. But we're still ahead of last year."

Getting into the radon-detection business can be as simple as buying a supply of kits and devising a marketing plan.

Existing labs like KSE can supply the tests themselves (metal canisters filled with radon-absorbing charcoal), and provide the results. The trick for you, the entrepreneur, is to find the right marketing strategy. Some companies sell test kits by mail or through retail outlets, and have customers send in for the results themselves. Others place the kits in homes, pick them up, and mail them in for testing. Quinlan reports that some companies have even branched out into remedial work, making them truly full-service operations.

The first step, according to Quinlan, is to map out a plan. From there, the business is fairly easy to learn. "The most difficult part of the business is advertising," he says. "You have to know enough about radon to educate your customers, but you don't have to be a scientific genius. We provide the lab expertise."

INTERIOR DESIGN

Business:

Designing attractive, functional interiors for homes and offices, retail shops, restaurants, etc.; also, coordinating vendors and supervising installations for design projects

Basic Equipment and Expenses:

$8,000

Necessities:

Telephone, transportation, drafting equipment

Experience Required:

Experience in the field or training from a community college or adult education program worthwhile

Inside Tip:

Before you launch your business, take on a project for free. The experience you gain will help you decide whether or not this business is right for you. And if the results are good, you'll have a reference and material for your portfolio.

"Most of my job is problem-solving—dealing with people and trying to get them to do the things they're supposed to do," says Garland, Texas, interior designer Joyce Schiska. "Everybody seems to think that interior designers have such a glamorous life, but it's very hard work and very detailed. The design end of it is fun, but that isn't twenty-four-hours a day. That's just a small part of what a designer does."

If Schiska's statement has shattered all your illusions about the artsy, creative field of interior design, so be it. You might as well know the truth now. But if you have an eye for design, a mind for details, and you're ready to get down to business, this could be just the opportunity you're looking for. Designers who have been in business less than two years generally handle between 20 and 40 small- or medium-sized projects a year and gross between $300,000 and $500,000. With net profits averaging between 10 and 20 percent, interior design isn't a bad way to make a living—even if it doesn't make for a life of non-stop glamour.

As a designer, your overriding goal is to create beautiful and functional working or living environments. What that means in plain English is that you'll be mapping out floor plans, putting together color schemes, lining up suppliers, supervising installations, and reporting to your clients. A typical day might find you figuring out where to place electrical outlets or deciding how to alter existing plumbing facilities to accommodate a new bathtub.

Most design work falls into two categories: commercial and residential. According to the designers we spoke with, commercial design is the more lucrative field. Contract design (which does not include all commercial projects but only those on which a designer must bid) is a $47 billion market.

On the other hand, residential design may offer pockets of opportunity to the small operator that commercial design does not. While most interior designers specialize in either commercial or residential work, it is possible to do both and double your potential market.

If you're starting from scratch in this field, try to get some hands-on experience or classes under your belt before jumping into the business. Once you've mastered the basic skills, the main challenge is marketing. "I'm marketing every phone call and every cocktail party, everywhere I go," says Alan Lucas of Alan Lucas & Associates, Inc. in Mountain View, California. "Business is not going to just fall over on your doorstep," he continues. "You have to make it happen."

For More Information:

Institute of Business Designers
1155 Merchandise Mart
Chicago, IL 60654-1104
(312) 467-1950

American Society of Interior Designers
1430 Broadway
New York, NY 10018
(212) 944-9220

HANDYMAN SERVICE

Business:

Doing all varieties of light repair, from fixing a leaky faucet to hanging a new painting; may also do odd jobs like putting up fences or installing irrigation systems. As handyman Jim Marley puts it, "anything that doesn't require a license."

Basic Equipment and Expenses:

$3,000

Necessities:

Telephone, transportation, tools (a varied supply is required, but can be bought as needed)

Experience Required:

No set licensing requirements, but must be handy with tools and good with people

Inside Tip:

Be punctual. If you're running late on a job, be sure to call and let your client know. "People understand if you call, but they get upset if you don't," says handyman Marley.

Where home repairs are concerned, it's the little things that get you: the sticky door, the jammed window, the toilet that never stops running. You don't call a contractor—or a full-fledged plumber—for these kinds of projects. But you can't always handle them yourself.

Or can you? If you're handy around the house, the rest of the population has a job for you. As the population ages in America, the need for basic "handyman" services is on the rise. Add to that the demand from working couples who don't have the time to do odd jobs (or who never learned how to in the first place), and you'll see the potential in this low-investment, high-profit business. Handyman services aren't new, they're just experiencing new growth.

Jim Marley, owner of Help-U-Fix in Mission Viejo, California, started doing minor repairs part-time in 1981. Initially, a friend needed help fixing up some property and asked Marley to lend a hand. Since that friend was in the real-estate business, that project led to more. "During the final inspection [before a house is sold], there's always something that needs to be fixed," Marley says. "If there was something I couldn't do, I'd find someone else who could. That would save the customer some hassle."

Two years ago, Marley realized that his part-time venture had full-time potential. So he quit his job as a computer programmer, and hasn't looked back since. "I saw it as a way to get off the freeway and do something I really like to do," he says. "I've always liked working with my hands. People were always asking me to help out on one thing or another."

Marley has had no problem filling his calendar. Once, he distributed flyers to residents of a senior citizen's community. That brought in so much business, he hasn't had to do any formal advertising in a year. "It's like anything else," he says. "You tell people what you do and they say, 'I know someone who needs that kind of service!' It's the old networking game."

In addition to networking, Marley considers customer service his greatest marketing tool. Common courtesy, it seems, is rare among home-service people. Marley makes it a point to be considerate and professional. "If people call, I call them back," he says. "So many people out there don't return phone calls when they're busy. I think that's burning bridges. If I can't do a job right away, I just explain that I'm busy. Most people are willing to wait. If they can't, sometimes I'll refer them to someone else, so that one way or another we get the job done."

Provided you're responsible and fairly adept with your hands, starting a handyman business is relatively simple. The main expense in this business is tools. "You need a variety of tools," he says. "It's not like being a carpenter, where you can get away with maybe a hammer and some saws and so on. You need plumbing tools and irrigation tools and all sorts of different tools." For the first six years, Marley put a good percentage of his earnings into tools. In total, he estimates that he's spent $5,000 on equipment. You don't have to buy everything before you start, though. "As I need something, I'll go out and buy it," he says.

FURNITURE REFINISHING

Business:

Repairing and refinishing wood furniture

Basic Equipment and Expenses:

$10,000

Necessities:

Telephone, refinishing equipment and supplies

Experience Required:

Learn refinishing techniques from books, classes, or seminars

Inside Tip:

Veteran refinisher Wade Wooten suggests using water-based
materials rather than traditional lacquers. They're safer and
cheaper to insure.

Furniture refinishing is a venerable old art that's enjoying
new popularity as Americans rediscover the value of older
furniture. "People are realizing that the quality they're getting today isn't what they were getting before," says Wade
Wooten of Wooten's Refinishing in Austin, Texas. "Even pieces
from the thirties, forties, and fifties are of much higher
quality than the stuff they're making today. And we can make
these pieces look better than they did in the showroom in
1950."

Wooten has been a professional refinisher since 1983.
Before that, he pursued it strictly as a hobby, picking up
knowledge informally from craftsmen around the world. He

started the business in a storage building behind his house. He considered it a logical offshoot of the family antique shop. Over the years, however, he's expanded the business to include as many as eight employees working on everything from "Grandma's rocker" to government and commercial accounts.

According to Wooten, being a crack refinisher requires a lot of detailed knowledge. The antiques Wooten deals with can be centuries old: He has to know what the original finish was, whether or not that finish has been redone in the interim, and what new products might work best. In order to do a conscientious job, you have to be a true craftsperson.

At the same time, Wooten observes, you have to achieve a certain volume to stay in business. Wooten manages both by sticking to a strict production schedule. "The trick is to apply production-line techniques to old-world materials and techniques," he says.

To start, Wooten suggests serious marketing. "You need to spend as much time visiting interior designers and antique shows as you do learning the production end," he says. Moreover, make sure you like the work before you get into it. "I turned my avocation into my vocation," he says. "I used to come home from work and start banging away on furniture. Now, I'm lucky enough to make that my business."

UPHOLSTERY REPAIR SERVICE

Business:

Repairing and re-upholstering furniture

Basic Equipment and Expenses:

$8,000

Necessities:

Industrial sewing machine, stapling system (electric or pneumatic), cutting table (ping-pong tables preferred), hand tools, shears, telephone. Licensing may be required: check your state government

Experience Required:

Must be a trained upholsterer. Instruction available through adult education and community college programs—or you may teach yourself by reading books, watching others, and practicing at home

Inside Tip:

Network with local refinishing shops to get job referrals and advertising tips.

Generally speaking, the same antique buffs that refinish their furniture also re-upholster it. Why? According to Tom Flanagan of Shingleton's Upholstery in Long Beach, California, people who re-upholster not only save money, but also preserve an irreplaceable item. "It's hard to be competitive with new furniture—the stuff they're making now is so cheap," says Flanagan. "But the quality isn't there. Something that was made twenty years ago is put together much better than what they're making today."

Upholstery businesses can take a variety of shapes. Karl Kunkel, editor of *The Professional Upholsterer* in High Point, North Carolina, reports that equipment costs start at about $2,500 for a home-based shop. Part-timers aren't uncommon in this business, and Kunkel says that moonlighting is a fine way to start. "You could start out of your living room," he says. "Your living room wouldn't look like much, but it can be done." Restoring home furniture seems to be the bulk of the business, though taking on commercial accounts or making accessories like decorative pillows are also an option. As you become more successful, you may even want to open a show-room.

The craft itself is relatively easy to learn. "It's not like calculus," Flanagan remarks. "I've been a pretty handy guy physically, so that hasn't been a problem for me." What's been more challenging is keeping up with the many respon-sibilities he faces as a shop owner. "I have to be here all the time," he says. "I have to take care of the phone, take care of the troops, take care of the customers—that's the downside. This is a labor-intensive business."

On the upside, though, it's possible to make a good living in the upholstery business if you "run it like a business, not like an upholsterer," in Flanagan's words. For all its ups and downs, Flanagan prefers running a business to his former work as an aerospace engineer. "Going from aerospace and dealing with the government to dealing with grandmothers and their needlepoint was traumatic," he laughs. "But at work you never really knew when you were going to get laid off, and I didn't like that."

HOME INSPECTION SERVICE

Business:

Inspecting home mechanical systems and structures for po-tential home buyers

Basic Equipment and Expenses:

$5,000

Necessities:

Telephone, transportation, ladder, flashlights, testing equip-ment

Experience Required:

Must have a solid understanding of home construction

Inside Tip:

Check out your trade association. The American Society of Home Inspectors in Washington, D.C., offers a variety of seminars, publications, and videos that can help you get your business off the ground.

Considering that an average home these days can cost upwards of $100,000, it's no wonder that home inspection services are gaining in popularity. In two to three hours, a professional home inspector can tell a prospective home buyer what's good—and not so good—about the property they want to buy.

"There's usually anywhere from $1,000 to $10,000 worth of problems that need to be repaired," says Towson, Maryland, home inspector John J. Heyn, president of the John Heyn Company and spokesperson for the American Society of Home Inspectors. "That information gives the buyers the opportunity to ask the seller to repair these problems, or to allow a credit for these repairs off the price of the house. At the very least, the buyer knows what he's getting into."

According to Heyn, a typical home inspection includes a check of all mechanical systems (plumbing, heating, electrical) and a once-over for any structural problems with walls, floors, ceilings, and roofs. To provide these services, a would-be inspector should have "a strong background in home construction or remodeling," says Heyn, as well as some training in the actual inspection process.

"Because home inspectors are held highly accountable in this business, I would advise them not to go into this business unless they have been well-trained in all aspects of inspection," Heyn says. "You have to have a good knowledge of how a house is put together to do a good job."

Heyn himself was in the construction business for years before he started doing professional home inspections in

1968. "Friends used to call me on the weekends to go see houses they were buying," he recalls. "Then their friends started calling me and offered to pay me for the inspections. I realized there was a need for this kind of service. I ran an ad, and people started calling right away." Today, Heyn's firm inspects homes, condominium complexes, apartment buildings, and commercial space—enough to keep ten professional inspectors busy.

Rates for two- or three-hour inspections range from $150 to $300. Heyn estimates that an inspector working alone can do two inspections a day comfortably, thereby bringing in gross sales of $75,000 or more annually.

To promote a new business, Heyn recommends advertising in the local paper and contacting real-estate agents in your area. Though the industry is growing, he maintains that there's still plenty of room for newcomers in this field. "In some parts of the country," he says, "as many as 50 percent of the people don't know about these services. That's a big potential market."

CHIMNEY SWEEPING

Business:

Cleaning and repairing chimneys

Basic Equipment and Expenses:

$5,000

Necessities:

Telephone, transportation, high-volume vacuum system, poles, brushes, hand tools for basic screening and masonry work

Experience Required:

Basic training essential, but relatively simple. Salesmanship is also important: Many clients must be educated on the value of a clean, safe chimney

Inside Tip:

Hire quality employees who can sell as well as perform the routine work. "They have to be able to run their mouths as well as clean the chimneys," says chimney sweep Ed Simonson.

Chimney sweeping isn't a new business, but it's enjoying renewed popularity today. Since the energy crisis of the seventies, Americans have grown fonder of their fireplaces. Consequently, they're paying more attention to chimney maintenance—and with good reason. A poorly maintained chimney can catch fire and cause a whole house to burn down. Moreover, structural problems can cause a chimney to crack or crumble, especially if the situation goes unnoticed for years.

Hence the need for America's estimated 6,000 chimney sweeps. Fort Worth, Texas, entrepreneur Ed Simonson says he's seen this business go "from people flogging flues to a regular technological industry" during his eleven years in business. Sales at Simonson's Top Hat Chimney Sweep reached $500,000 in 1987. Even with the recent economic downturn in northern Texas, Simonson's service is holding strong.

Simonson got into the chimney-sweeping business in 1978 after quitting his job in a huff. "I said then that I wasn't going to work for anyone anymore even if I had to clean barns," he recalls. But Simonson had a wife and baby to support, and after months of cashing in CD accounts and letting magazine subscriptions run out, things began to look bleak. "Every business I saw took thousands of dollars to start," Simonson says. "I was looking for a bootstrap business." While browsing the pages of the *Mother Earth News* (fatefully, the one subscription that hadn't been canceled), Simonson came across an article on chimney sweeping. He was so intrigued, he stayed up all night reading about it. When his wife came downstairs to feed the baby at four A.M., Simonson said he was going to be a chimney sweep. Sleepily, she said, "Fine."

"I had the go-ahead," Simonson laughs.

Over the next few years, Simonson learned all about chimneys. He ordered cleaning equipment and learned how to use it. Then, he gave away ten free cleanings to get a feel for the work. His first cleaning took him three hours. Once he got up to speed, he could clean a chimney in thirty minutes. Simonson also learned everything he could about the chimneys themselves—how they were built, which problems to look for. He found that a high percentage of chimneys needed repair. They were improperly installed or made of inferior materials. In time, he started offering repairs as well, and from there the business really took off.

Today, three full-time chimney sweeps handle Simonson's rounds, while he attends to administration and marketing. Simonson's employees must undergo a month's training, pass a certification test, and show considerable sales ability to stay on the job. "If all an employee is going to do is clean chimneys, I can't keep them," says Simonson. "These guys are out there selling our company. That's how we make money, and how they make money too."

Simonson estimates that an aspiring chimney sweeper should budget $2,500 to $5,000 to start up a new firm. Equipment, a business phone, and some local advertising are the primary expenses. He also recommends that a new business owner spend as much time as possible educating him- or herself about the business. While learning enough to get started won't take long, understanding the nuances of the business will. "You're going to spend more on education during your first three years than anything else," Simonson contends. In the long run, that knowledge will pay off in a solid reputation and a loyal following.

Otherwise, his advice is simply to get your feet wet. "You work hard and you educate yourself to the best of your abil-

ity," he urges. "Jump in with both feet and start stroking. It's
the same advice I'd give to anyone in any endeavor. Don't do it
part time; jump in and make it work."

For More Information:

Copperfield Chimney Supply
Attn: Marketing
304 South 20th Street
Fairfield, Iowa 52556
(515) 472-4126
Publishes *Chimney Chatter*, a newsletter on the chimney
maintenance business.

ROOMS TO GROW

> Mark Booren isn't an architect or a contractor, but he's the next
> best thing. For Colorado do-it-yourselfers, Booren fills the gap
> between going it alone and hiring a team of expensive profession-
> als.

Sometimes your ideal business doesn't exist. Mark
Booren knew there was a place for him in the growing remodeling field. But he wasn't a contractor, he wasn't an
architect, and he wasn't an interior designer.

No clearly defined position existed for Booren in the remodeling industry, so he fashioned his own. Booren's Denver, Colorado, company, The Papillon Group, helps clients
put their remodeling plans into action. "I consult with homeowners about changes they want completed and draw up the
plans for their comments," he explains. "I do the preliminary
work that an architect does, but for a fraction of the cost."
After clients approve his plans, Booren runs them by a real
architect and engineer to make sure everything is in order.

"Once we decide on a final plan, and I have collected
estimates from subcontractors, we move ahead with the con-

struction," Booren says. Booren also supervises construction, making sure that the job is done on time and within budget—two factors that often go awry when homeowners try to do things themselves. Since he launched the business in 1987, Booren has taken on all sorts of projects—from hanging wallpaper to remodeling entire homes.

Booren's background doesn't exactly point toward his current business. Before starting The Papillon Group, he was a commercial fisherman and chairman of a seafood marketing company in Alaska. He caught the remodeling bug when he moved to Colorado and remodeled his own home. "I saw the need for someone who would fall somewhere between a do-it-yourselfer and a general contractor," he says. Shortly thereafter, he became that person.

Booren learned the design end of the business by reading architectural and design books. But most of his expertise comes from clients, not from training. "You have to get inside people's heads and find out what they want," he says. "I can't sell someone my designs, but I can produce designs according to what they tell me." He borrows the technical skills from consultants—many of whom are retired professionals. Even the drafting is done by a retired architect.

According to Booren, the remodeling industry is ripe with opportunity—even in slow economic times. Booren started his business in the midst of Denver's oil crisis. "Everybody said I was crazy doing it," he says, "but I figured everybody wants to improve their lot in life. New home building had dropped off to nothing here in Denver. People who wanted to upgrade their homes—or add rooms for new children—had to think about remodeling."

9

THE PERSONAL TOUCH

PERSONAL SHOPPER

Business:

Buying clothes, gifts, groceries, specialty items, and other sundry goods for busy individual and corporate clients

Basic Equipment and Expenses:

$3,500

Necessities:

Transportation, telephone with an answering machine

Experience Required:

Passion for shopping, familiarity with local shops and mail order catalogs, good taste

Inside Tip:

In addition to taking on clients, try contracting with various stores. You'll be able to boost their sales by offering a service other stores don't.

No question about it: Shopping is a skill. That's why two people can emerge from the same January clearance sale with entirely different experiences. The amateur is bewildered, breathless, unable to think. The pro emerges with armloads of loot—everything he or she needs for next year's Christmas gifts—ready to sit down with a cup of coffee and back issues of the L.L. Bean catalog. Where shopping is concerned, some people have it and others don't.

If you were born to shop, you can turn your talents into a profitable business. While you may not consider shopping work, others definitely do—and they're willing to pay you good money to do that work for them.

"Many people like to buy personal gifts but are unable to get out and do it, or they have a hard time making good choices," says Antonia Flitner, owner of Preferred Stock shopping service in Santa Rosa, California. "I'm shopping constantly—I always have been—for my friends and family, so my business and personal interests mesh." Because they're professionals, personal shoppers zero in on the right stuff more efficiently than plain folks. For corporate clients, the cost of hiring a personal shopper is actually less than sending out an inexperienced secretary—not to mention the morale savings.

What do personal shoppers buy? Pretty much anything, according to the businesses we spotted. Steve Martin, owner of Groceries To You! in Chicago, delivers just that: groceries. His clients—mainly busy urban professionals—just don't have the time to market. Other popular items are gifts (for relatives, friends, clients, and business associates), clothes, and unusual items. One shopper was charged with the task of finding chocolate toothpaste. Professional that she was, she found it.

Flexibility is one of the main advantages of this business. Working from home is ideal to start since very little of your business will take place in your office. Limiting your work to part-time is also a possibility, which means you can keep your current job while you're building a steady client base. Best of all, this is one of the few businesses where your talents as a shopper can really shine.

NAIL SALON

Business:

Doing manicures and pedicures, either in your own salon or as a subcontractor in a larger salon

Basic Equipment and Expenses:

$7,000 for an independent salon; $2,000 for an inside station

Necessities:

Tables, chairs, lighting, miscellaneous nail care products, supplies, and equipment

Experience Required:

Must be a trained, licensed nail technician; training available at most beauty schools

Inside Tip:

Check demand for nail care services in your area before opening an independent salon. In some neighborhoods, salons exist on every corner. Shop around for an area that needs your services.

In the last five years or so, manicures have made a comeback. And why not? Nail care is one of the most affordable luxuries around.

And it's also one of the most accessible businesses open to new entrepreneurs. In order to start a nail salon, you must be trained as a nail technician. Programs at most beauty colleges last anywhere from three to three and a half months (350 hours), and cover such subjects as chemistry, physiology, aesthetics, sterilization, bacteriology, and even a little psychology.

According to El Toro, California, nail technician Pat Nation, chairman of the Nail Technicians of America (NTA), professionalism and personality are the marks of a good artist. "I educate my clients new and old," she says. "I get a full medical history. I ask them about their activities and their lifestyles. I try to do their nails according to the shape of their hands and the colors they like to wear." She also cultivates good relations with clients. "The personal relationships you build with clients are important," she notes. "Twenty years after I started, I still have regular customers who come to see me."

Nation once owned an independent shop, but now subcontracts from a salon called The Village Ritz. Though she enjoyed having her own salon, she reports that her current arrangement enables her to pursue outside work—including educational work for the NTA. As a subcontractor, she says, "you can set your own hours and your own goals."

As in most businesses, the early months are the toughest. To establish a new clientele, Nation suggests choosing a location with a lot of foot traffic and putting your friends at the top of your client list. Referrals from them should start generating business.

Nation observes that many areas have nail salons on every corner—many of which are not run by licensed professionals. While these operations may be here today, Nation isn't sure they will be tomorrow. In the long run, quality service and sound business principles should prevail. That's why she stresses that basic training and continuing education are critical in this business. "Anybody can be mediocre," she says. "But it doesn't take any more effort to do things right." Ultimately, it may be the best business decision you'll make.

PERSONAL TRAINING

Business:

Working one-on-one with aspiring fitness buffs. May include weight training, aerobics, running, walking—or virtually any sport

Basic Equipment and Expenses:

$2,500

Necessities:

Transportation, telephone. If the sport you're coaching requires equipment, you'll need that as well

Experience Required:

Expertise in general fitness and some aspect of sports required. The more you know about physiology, nutrition, and sports injuries, the better

Inside Tip:

In addition to individual clients, look for work in the corporate market. By signing on offices full of executives, you can fill your schedule faster and more efficiently.

The mind is willing, but the flesh is weak. In a perfect world, we would all make it to the gym three times a week. Our motivation would never flag; we would never get stuck in traffic. And we'd never be tempted to cheat on our sit-ups, arm curls, or thirty-minute ride on the Lifecycle.

But in the real world, people need help keeping their intended exercise schedules. For those who can afford one, a personal trainer can help achieve that goal.

As a business, personal training offers a raft of unique benefits. For one thing, you need virtually nothing but clients to get started. Since the whole point of personal training is to work around the clients' lives, most of your work will take place at their location, not yours. Moreover, there are no complicated requirements for becoming a trainer. You should be fit (flab will destroy your credibility), and you should have some knowledge of fitness and sports. But if you're a fitness fanatic now, you probably have a lot of the background you need already. And what better way to keep yourself motivated to work out than to be paid for doing it?

Personal trainer Jim Gisondo started his Santa Monica, California-based business, Dynamic Bodies, in 1983. "I was a bodybuilder and I loved weight training," he says. "To me, it's one of the best forms of exercise you can do." Gisondo works out individualized exercise programs for clients that include a combination of weight training, aerobics, and floor exercises. Gisondo also sells weight-training equipment, so that clients can set up their own home workout centers if they like.

If this sounds like pretty high-class stuff, it's no mistake. Personal trainers attract an affluent clientele. Hourly rates around the Los Angeles area, for example, run as high as $250. Gisondo charges a relatively modest $50 an hour. Moreover, he will also make an effort to work within more modest budgets. "I feel I need to put something back into the health field," he says. "If someone seriously wants to improve themselves through exercise, I'll try to help them out in terms of price."

Most of his clients, however, need no such price breaks. For the dozen or so individual and corporate clients Gisondo works with, convenience and personalized service are worth the extra price. "At health clubs, everybody gets the same program," Gisondo explains, "but not everybody is going to respond to the same thing. I work out a program especially for each client. If someone is serious about getting fit, they want to do it the right way." Gisondo reports that it takes him a month to figure out all of a client's idiosyncracies and adjust his program to fit those requirements.

Gisondo's advice to would-be trainers is to "practice what they preach" and maintain a high level of personal fitness, and to learn as much as possible about the health and fitness fields. "This business encompasses a lot more than working out," he says. "You can never learn enough."

VCR INSTALLATION AND TRAINING

Business:

On-site installation of VCR machines; training clients to program and use machines

Basic Equipment and Expenses:

$2,500

Necessities:

Tool box, transportation, phone with answering machine/answering service

Experience Required:

Knack for working with electronics (formal electronics training not necessary), people skills

Inside Tip:

Because referrals are essential in this business, customer

service is a priority. Pay as much attention to your personal approach as you do to your technical skills.

Considering that literally millions of American households own VCR machines, you'd think that programming and installing a VCR would have become as simple as turning on the TV. But that simply isn't the case, according to John Korczynski of Austin, Texas. Since 1987, Korczynski's House Calls—A VCR Service has been hooking up local VCRs and educating owners on the finer points of programming.

"Some people could take two weeks to figure out how to hook up their machines on their own," says Korczynski. "Some people couldn't figure it out even if you gave them two weeks. There are a lot of ways to program a VCR, but unless you know how to operate the equipment, it's just a big hunk of plastic."

Hence the need for a video set-up service. For a flat fee of $25, Korczynski travels to customers' homes and gets their machines up and running. He also teaches clients all about their VCRs—how to program, what kind of tape to buy, and how to maintain the machines. Korczynski doesn't do any repairs, just installation and training.

Though having a knack with electronics helps, no formal training is necessary. In fact, Korczynski points out that none is available. Practicing on friends' machines and learning on the job taught him everything he knows. And most VCR machines come with instruction manuals.

Equipment costs for this business are minimal. Basic tools, wires, switches, and a television monitor are all Korczynski uses. Transportation is necessary, but it needn't be fancy: "All I needed when I started out was a vehicle," says Korczynski, "and mine was a clunker."

The only other start-up expense is the phone. While hiring a receptionist or answering service is a nice option, an answering machine works just fine.

Korczynski schedules a maximum of four appointments per day, spending an average of one to three hours on each call. Though he admits that he could do a cursory installation in a fraction of that time (and thereby increase his volume), he refuses to rush.

"With some people, it just takes a little longer for the information to set in," he says. "I have a set rate no matter how long it takes. I want people to be satisfied with the work I do. If they aren't happy—if they feel they've been cheated—they won't recommend me to their relatives or friends."

Word of mouth is Korczynski's best advertising, so customer service is his first priority. He credits his success to "being able to meet people face to face and make them feel comfortable. Remember, I'm asking people to let me into their homes. If they don't feel comfortable around me, they're not going to feel good about what I've done. I'm just a simple country boy and I don't put on any front. By the time I leave, I'm like part of the family."

Korczynski plans to expand his business with a stereo set-up service. Though friends and clients have urged him to offer repairs and maintenance on VCR units as well, Korczynski has resisted. "I went into this business to work with people," he says. "I don't want to do work at home."

As far as Korczynski knows, there are only a few VCR set-up services in the country. To find out if your area could support such a service, ask around at appliance stores in your neighborhood—or take out an inexpensive ad in the local paper. Korczynski got his start by answering a letter in a newspaper advice column. Two weeks after his name and number ran, he had nine months worth of bookings.

IMAGE CONSULTING

Business:

Helping clients find the right look—including advice on clothes, accessories, hairstyles, cosmetics, and so on

Basic Equipment and Expenses:

$10,000

Necessities:

Telephone, marketing brochures/flyers

Experience Required:

None, though training in image consulting is available and recommended. Most image consultants come from backgrounds in fashion merchandising, design, public relations, or cosmetology

Inside Tip:

Before you get started, make sure you know your stuff. Read up on the business, attend seminars, and visit a few image consultants yourself.

Looks can kill. If you don't believe it, try attending your next business meeting in a Hawaiian shirt and shorts. Since we were first told to "dress for success" in the seventies, Americans have been trying to find the right look—and often struggling in the process.

It's precisely this dilemma that's made image consulting a successful industry. Brenda York, president of the Academy of Fashion and Image in McLean, Virginia, estimates that Americans spend some $148 million on image-consulting services a year. Established consultants gross as much as $100,000 to $200,000 a year, a fair return on a relatively low initial investment.

Image consulting as we know it began with color analysis. In the early eighties, it was a revelation to have one's colors "done." But now, image consultants do much more than suggest the right colors to wear. "The seasonal color [trend] has reached its peak," says York. "We have to look at what's next." Among the skills that York considers critical: producing fashion shows, coaching etiquette and protocol, and working with both male and female clients.

Ed and Ellen Drwal of Drwal & Associates in Cleveland, Ohio, have twenty years of management experience between them. Ed feels this experience is crucial in providing his clients with the image information they need. Drwal & Associates offers its clients a one-hour color analysis for $45 and a complete three-hour image analysis for $125, which includes color analysis, a wardrobe checklist, and body shape, face shape, and hairstyle analysis.

Considering today's image-conscious society, now is the time to start an image-consulting business. But it takes more than a telephone and a few hours of training to get established as an image consultant.

Marketing your image service will take a lot of time, especially in the beginning. First, decide whom you should target as potential clients—recent college graduates, working women, corporate executives, etc. Then, decide on a format for your sessions. Should they be private three-hour consultations, or day-long seminars? How many people should attend at one time? How much should you charge? (Typical image consulting fees range from $50 to $250 an hour. An all-day fee might run between $500 and $2,000.)

Once you have a good idea of how your business will run, there are a number of ways to get your name known. For starters, don't be afraid to contact every professional you know, or anyone else who might be interested in your services. Investing in well-designed business cards, letterhead stationery, and a four-color brochure is a good idea.

Don't forget that location can play an important role in image consulting. Many consultants work out of their homes and do very well. A down-the-road option is renting a small office in a downtown location. This may encourage corporate clients to come to you, since you're "in the neighborhood" and therefore perceived as a professional.

DATING SERVICE

Business:
Matchmaking for money

Basic Equipment and Expenses:
$7,500

Necessities:
Telephone, advertising, home computer highly recommended

Experience Required:
None. People skills are, naturally, very important

Inside Tip:
Place ads in the personal sections of local papers and regional magazines to reach your target market.

Meeting the right person has always been one of life's great trials. But in today's career-oriented world, it may be more difficult than ever. People who spend twelve hours a day at the office don't have time to go out and mingle with strangers. Yet many offices frown on employees dating each other. Even married people aren't immune: About half of all marriages end in divorce. And even good marriages end with one or the other partner being widowed.

Mary Ann Siersdale, co-owner of Lunch Couples in Needham, Massachusetts, notes that the matchmaking market has never been stronger. Lunch Couples has over one thousand active members with no slowdown in sight. "We cater to all age groups and all professions," she says. Some of her clients are in their seventies.

Why the surge in interest? "The dating business has changed from the lonely-hearts club image it used to have," says David Siersdale, Mary Ann's partner and husband. "We deal with people who want to meet the right person, but don't know where. They realize they need help." And according to David, singles aren't necessarily demanding a lot of frills. "They don't really want the cutesy stuff like computer dating or video dating," he says. "They just want to meet someone appropriate."

Lunch Couples offers just that. Clients sign up over the phone. They undergo an extensive interview, indicate the kind of person they'd like to meet, and send in photos. From there, the Lunch Couples staff matches them with people they think might be compatible. If the prospective couple agrees, a lunch date is made. Mary Ann stresses that this nonthreatening arrangement has been critical to their success. "They go to the meeting in their own cars and they meet during the day," she says. "No addresses are given out, so there's very little risk."

There's also little risk in the prices. A year's membership costs less than $500—just a fraction of what some of the swankier organizations charge. Three-month and six-month arrangements are also available. Mary Ann estimates that in a year, a typical client will meet twenty people, one of whom may well be the perfect match. "We've had numerous marriages and long-term relationships come about as the result of our services," she says. "It's a very satisfying business."

It's also lucrative. "We bring in over $100,000 a year out of our breezeway," Mary Ann jokes. The Siersdales started the business in 1982 with little more than a phone, some interview forms, and several ads in local newspapers and magazines. Not only did they get calls from clients, they also got calls from the media. "We had a lot of interest for stories," Mary Ann says. "The idea of romance is very appealing."

As the business has grown, the Siersdales have delegated many of the day-to-day operations to their staff. Mary Ann currently puts in about twenty hours a week. Additionally, they do consulting with new dating services in other towns.

"We have manuals with information on how to run the business, and we give them a week's training here in Needham," says Mary Ann. She reports that while the business looks simple, it does require a certain flair for matchmaking. The Siersdales are solid supporters of their own methods. They started the business as friends and ended up married. "We're our own best success story," David says.

ERRAND SERVICE

Business:

Handling the scores of personal errands that working people don't have time to handle themselves

Basic Equipment and Expenses:

$3,000

Necessities:

Telephone, transportation, insurance; a home computer is helpful

Experience Required:

Ability to juggle many tasks at once; knowing how to run a household is a good start

Inside Tip:

This is the kind of timely business that gets local press coverage. Write up an informative, lively press release on your service and send it to the local media: Free publicity could well be the result.

Many of us grew up in homes artfully managed by homemakers. Usually, that homemaker was Mom. She would cook, clean, grocery shop, balance the family checkbook, wait for the plumber, cart the dog to the vet and the kids to school, stand in line at the post office or the bank. At the time, it was hard to appreciate all the errands and responsibilities that Mom shouldered. But now, for the millions of American families without full-time homemakers, Mom is sorely missed.

Alas, one can never buy another Mom. But, thanks to services like Lois Barnett's P.S. Personalized Services in Chicago, consumers can hire the next best thing. Barnett's service takes over the "boring details of [clients'] lives." In Barnett's words, "We'll find it, we'll do it, we'll wait for it."

Barnett started the business out of her home. She offers a variety of everyday services—from shopping for groceries to teaching clients how to use their home computers. There's no shortage of work: more than thirty clients regularly call upon Barnett's services. And surprisingly, there's been no shortage of help either. Barnett's employees are generally bright, capable, "overqualified" individuals who are tired of the corporate rut.

Though this business doesn't require any particular experience or training, you must be reliable, efficient, and conscientious to succeed. "Of course, we're insured and bonded," Barnett explains, "but in this kind of business the key is to be personally recommended or, in the initial contact, to communicate to a potential client that we're trustworthy."

PERFECT FIT

Buying a Jazzercise franchise gave aerobics instructor Francesca Sanders the tools she needed to build her own "community" of fitness buffs.

It wasn't entrepreneurial zeal that drove Jazzercise instructor Francesca Sanders into business for herself: It was the desire to make a difference. "I had been about ninety pounds heavier than I am now," she explains. "I wanted to start teaching to show people that it can be done. Five percent of the people out there have perfect bodies and exercise to keep them that way. The rest of us think, 'If I could just get rid of these big thighs, I'd be okay.' Some instructors focus on who can kick the highest or sweat the most. I'm glad that my students come to class. I don't care what their bodies look like. I want their hearts to work, so they can be healthy."

If Sanders sounds like a believer, she is. She decided to try Jazzercise—reluctantly—after seeing founder Judi Sheppard Missett on the Phil Donahue Show. "I had never exercised in my life," she says. In short order, she was hooked. Ninety pounds later, she figured she had a unique perspective on fitness to share with fellow students and decided to strike out on her own. In 1984, she bought a Jazzercise franchise and started teaching classes in West Hollywood, California.

Sanders provides the enthusiasm and a wicked, incessant wit that makes all the leg lifts and aerobics bearable. Jazzercise, on the other hand, offers "a million things" that Sanders couldn't get independently.

For one thing, there's the program itself. "In eight years of doing Jazzercise, I've never had an injury," Sanders says. Having a set program also frees her up to pursue outside interests like lecturing on children's fitness, teaching at local elementary schools, choreographing halftime numbers for sporting events, and taking cardio-funk dance classes.

Sanders also considers the networking opportunities she has as a Jazzercise franchisee important. "I don't have the kinds of concerns that most aerobics instructors have," she says. "Other instructors talk about teaching classes when they're injured. I would never do that." Another Jazzercise instructor is usually available to fill in when she's unable to teach. "Also, I have someone to call when a routine isn't working for me," she notes. "If you work at a club, you probably don't know anyone else who's doing the same program."

And, of course, being her own boss is fairly rewarding as well. "When you teach at a health club, you're paid so many dollars to teach a class, and it doesn't matter whether there are three people there or fifty," she observes. "You're not really rewarded for being a good instructor. I have a real incentive to do a good job." Students appreciate that dedication, too. "They know this is Francesca's class," she says. "They know I'll be here, that I'm not going to get another job for two dollars more an hour."

Sanders describes herself as "not making a million dollars," but she adds that she's making at least as much as she would working full-time at a regular job. The early months, reportedly, were rough. "I put flyers up everywhere," she says, "in every legal place and every illegal place. I stood in front of libraries and supermarkets. I dropped them into open windows."

The first classes were small—sometimes nonexistent— but if Sanders has one strength, it's relating to people. Even now, she considers her best "marketing" tool the ability to keep students coming to her classes—and bringing their friends. Personal postcards are a monthly ritual, and inviting whole classes over for Sunday brunch is not unheard of. Today, she teaches about 150 students per month in five weekly classes. "Some nights I might make $300, other nights I might make $28," she says. "It all balances out in the end."

Perhaps the most rewarding aspect of the business for Sanders is creating a sense of community among her students. In addition to their regular workouts, Sanders encourages them to pull together to collect food for the homeless, or funds for the American Heart Association.

"The aerobic industry is so focused on the body," she says. "Instead, what we should be doing is working with whole people. We should be reaching out to the people who come to class for the first time and feel like clods. We should be making them feel good about exercising and good about themselves. When you focus on the size of a person's biceps or who's the best dancer, and you make your classes so hard that most people can't keep up, you're really missing the boat. If you can create an atmosphere where people can come and feel like they're doing something positive for themselves, you reach a lot more people."

10

TOP DOGS AND FAT CATS

Aquarium Service

Business:

Designing, installing, cleaning, and maintaining aquariums

Basic Equipment and Expenses:

$2,500

Necessities:

Transportation, telephone, basic tools for cleaning aquariums, water-testing kits. Actual aquariums, equipment, and fish to be installed may be purchased at time of sale

Experience Required:

Must be knowledgeable about all kinds of fish and aquarium-related products

Inside Tip:

Team up with an existing aquarium shop. In exchange for their referrals, offer them a commission and/or agree to buy all your materials from them at retail prices. The exposure you get will be invaluable—probably cheaper and more effective than advertising.

Who's minding the fish? It could be Jim Luyk of Tropical Seas, Inc., an aquarium service and retail tropical fish shop in Manhattan Beach, California, Tropical Seas provides a raft of services for aquarium owners—from designing and installing aquarium systems to providing monthly or bimonthly cleaning and maintenance.

According to Luyk, many would-be aquarium owners don't want to take the time and trouble to maintain their tanks. Moreover, consumers can have a hard time learning about fish care, especially where exotic saltwater fish are concerned. "The information out there is hard to obtain," Luyk says. "You'll get different information at each store, usually depending on the salesperson's personal experience." With regular servicing, it's possible to enjoy an aquarium with virtually no effort at all. Luyk even sells electronic feeders that eliminate the need for daily meals.

Luyk's minimum charge for a service call is $35 for an hour's work. If the call requires overtime, he bills an additional $15 to $20. While he believes such prices aren't unreasonable for this kind of service, he also stresses that a serviceperson must know what he or she is doing to warrant the price. "If you make a mistake, you can collapse a whole tank," he says. "Sometimes, that means losing $200 or $300 worth of fish."

Perhaps the most difficult part of starting an aquarium service is finding clients. Luyk solved that problem by opening his own shop. "I get a lot of exposure through the shop," he says, while taking out an ad in the Yellow Pages cost more than it brought in. One option for newcomers is to negotiate with shopowners for referrals. Another is to launch the business part-time while you're still working and build a client base slowly by referral.

PET TAXI SERVICE

Business:

Shuttling dogs, cats, birds, rabbits, and other various fauna to the vet, the groomer, and other important appointments

Basic Equipment and Expenses:

$10,000

Necessities:

Van, station wagon, or similar vehicle for transport (used vehicle okay); cages, first-aid supplies, telephone with answering machine

Experience Required:

Must be good with animals

Inside Tip:

Advertise your service through local veterinarians, pet shops, and grooming salons

Here's a business that's going to the dogs—not to mention cats, birds, snakes, guinea pigs, and rabbits. Carting pets from place to place may sound like a frivolous business, but it's actually quite serious—and legitimate. Many pet owners can't accompany their pets to the vet's office or the grooming shop. They're either working or don't have adequate transportation.

These people can't call a regular limo, but they can call pet taxi services like Los Angeles entrepreneur Steve May's Pet Limo. May's motto is "We escort your pet to the vet," and that's precisely what he delivers. In addition to shuttling animals to routine appointments, May also offers twenty-four-hour emergency service. His air-conditioned van is equipped with fur-lined cages, stretchers, emergency road lights, and animal first-aid supplies.

May is a professional animal technician with fifteen years' experience. Over the years, he's had his share of nips and bites from perturbed pets. But hauling exotica such as monkeys, raccoons, boa constrictors, deer, billy goats, ducks, chickens, and a lion cub—not to mention everyday dogs, cats, and birds—doesn't faze May. In fact, he pipes in music to soothe the savage beasts. Classical, he claims, is the most soothing.

PET GROOMING

Business:

Bathing, clipping, and brushing dogs and, if you're ambitious, cats

Basic Equipment and Expenses:

$10,000

Necessities:

Telephone, workspace (see if your local ordinances will allow a homebased set-up), grooming table, cages, tub, clippers, combs, shampoo, ribbons

Experience Required:

Learn the grooming trade through a state-certified grooming school or hands-on through experience. Check with your local government to see if certification is required in your area

Inside Tip:

Buy a used van and offer mobile grooming, or pick-up and delivery.

Most people will do anything to get a dirty dog clean. Anything, that is, but wash it themselves. If you're good with animals and you don't mind getting your clothes wet, this could be the perfect business for you. Start-up costs are relatively low and the profits, reportedly, can be high. Rosemary and Carl Williams, co-owners of Dog Lovers in Los Angeles, predict sales of over $400,000 at their two locations in 1989.

Basic grooming at Dog Lovers includes a bath, flea dip, nail clipping, ear and teeth check, and a comb-out. Prices range from $19 to $45, depending on the type of dog. On the average, the grooming process takes an hour.

However, Dog Lovers hasn't become successful on basic grooming alone. They carry pet supplies, offer obedience training, and sell puppies. But perhaps the biggest brainstorm the Williams's had was to buy a van and offer mobile services. Until then, business at their shop was ho-hum. Once they hit the road, business picked up immediately.

"The problem wasn't that people didn't want their dogs groomed," says Rosemary. "It was getting their dogs to the shop. Often, people would say the dog was such a mess that they couldn't put him in the car because fleas would get all over the place. Or their dogs got carsick. So that's why we initiated the mobile service."

Depending on what's convenient for the owner, a dog can either be groomed on-site or brought back to the shop. It's not unusual to groom dogs in the van; in fact, Rosemary has even learned to enjoy it. "Having a dog alone in the van is nice because there aren't others barking and having fits," she says. On the other hand, some dogs are too much to handle in a confined space. "We try not to do chows in the van, for example," says Carl. "That gets to be too hard."

DOG TRAINING

Business:

Teaching all dogs new tricks: focusing on behavior problems, basic obedience, and protection training

Basic Equipment and Expenses:

$2,500

Necessities:

Telephone, transportation, advertising/brochures

Experience Required:

Training in dog training is essential (this is not the same as teaching your own dog to sit), communication skills, marketing ability. Also, you must love dogs

Inside Tip:

Get your business free publicity by sending an article on dog-training tips to the local newspaper. One topic idea: "Ten Most Common Dog Training Mistakes."

According to Los Angeles dog trainer Matthew Margolis, there are 50 million dogs in America, but only a handful of good trainers. And that includes dog owners themselves.

"Ninety-nine percent of all dog owners need help," he says. "When someone has their first baby, they don't know how to take care of it. They need a support group of doctors and friends and family to teach them. So why should they know how to train a dog? If the dog is scared of them, if they're angry at the dog all the time, they need a trainer."

Margolis and his staff of thirty train some 3,000 dogs a year through his National Institute of Dog Training. In addition to appearing on the *Tonight Show*, Margolis has authored six books on dog behavior and training and has three new books in the hopper. He learned dog training over twenty years ago from an East Coast dog trainer, and began his own practice in 1968. "I pioneered the idea of at-home training," he says. "Most of the training at that time was in classes or in kennels. I went right to people's homes and worked with the dogs there."

While Margolis believes that home is a perfect environment for dogs to learn, training dogs on-site also eliminates the need for a business location. Working from a home office, a trainer can build his or her business by contacting veterinarians, dog groomers, pet stores, and by advertising in the local paper.

At the National Institute of Dog Training, rates for a six-week (one hour per week) course start at $695. Though the demand for these services is clearly there, Margolis emphasizes that being a qualified trainer is critical to success. He recommends reading up on both dog training and animal behavior, and studying with an established trainer. Margolis, who teaches people to become trainers himself, urges potential dog trainers to find a good mentor. "There are a lot of bad trainers out there," he says. "Working with someone who uses a lot of negative methods won't do you any good."

What skills does a good trainer need? "Surely, you have to love dogs," he says. "You have to be patient, and you have to be good with people. Communication skills are important. And you have to have good work ethics—you have to show up on time and be conscientious." If you're good, says Margolis, people will come to you. "There's a tremendous need for good dog trainers," he says. "This industry is truly a sleeping giant."

DOG'S BEST FRIEND

Pet sitter Iris Rosenberg cooks breakfast, throws Frisbees, and watches television with her canine clients. "This is a business," she says, "though I have so much fun I sometimes wonder."

Iris Rosenberg guesses that most of her would-be competition is discouraged by the long hours and lack of holidays. "You have to work every weekend and every holiday," she says. Not to mention the eighteen-hour days.

What keeps Rosenberg going is not mere determination. She loves pets. Not in a cheap, casual kind of way—but earnestly. She cooks them bacon and eggs, takes them swimming, tunes in their favorite sitcoms or detective shows. She even sleeps over in a pinch (imagine her husband's surprise when she called to say, "I'm spending the night with Benjy"). Rosenberg is more than a pet sitter: She's a dog's best friend.

Since Rosenberg started Baltimore, Maryland's Pet Sitters, Inc. in 1984, she has fed, exercised, and coddled a bevy of dogs, cats, rabbits, lizards, birds, tropical fish, and even wild animals. "I had been a legal secretary and a paralegal for sixteen years," Rosenberg says. "I wanted to get into a business working with animals. I had been dog sitting for a friend, and I thought, why not do the same for other people?"

Rosenberg launched her business while working at her former job. The attorneys she met through work became some of her first clients. From there, her business has grown largely through word-of-mouth and local publicity.

Of course, a reputation helps. Rosenberg's special rapport with animals speaks for itself. Whether she's coaxing a rabbit out of hiding or tossing a Frisbee with a canine client,

Rosenberg goes the extra mile. "I loved the business right away," she says. "It's really not like work to me." Owners like her style, too. "People have to give you the keys to their houses," she observes. "They want someone who's trustworthy, someone they feel comfortable with."

To start the business, Rosenberg didn't need a lot of equipment: just a phone, a car, and her trusty pet treats. Her biggest expense was liability insurance. She did, however, need a lot of time. "I'd advise people to have a good car and be prepared to drive everywhere when they first start out," she says. "The visits aren't really as time-consuming as the driving." In addition to her appointed rounds, Rosenberg spends roughly sixteen hours a week on paperwork. "That's the part I could do without," she says.

Pet Sitters's services encompass a variety of chores. Generally, Rosenberg (or one of her two regular contractors) visits cats once a day and dogs twice. She feeds and waters the animals. Cats get several minutes of in-house playtime. Dogs go for a brisk walk around the neighborhood or a run in a nearby park. Rosenberg also gives the house a daily once-over, bringing in the mail, turning lights on or off. Occasionally, she accepts straight house-sitting jobs. And sometimes, she exercises pets for clients who work all day. Her basic rate is $10 per visit, plus $2 for each additional pet, though she's planning a rate increase in the near future.

Rosenberg's biggest challenge is finding qualified help. The contractors she works with must be honest, dependable, good with animals, poised enough to go out on interviews, and must also own their own cars. Though she admits it's been difficult to find help, she also stresses that she'll need it to increase her volume.

The demand for services like Rosenberg's is certainly there: She works fifteen to eighteen hours a day, including weekends and holidays. Anyone who's had to drag a dog yelping and yowling all the way to the vet's knows why. Vacationing customers also appreciate having someone come by the house while they're gone. In fact, Rosenberg once walked in on a burglary. She grabbed the dog and the phone, then dialed the police.

Rosenberg admits that her business isn't for everyone. But it's hard to imagine a business more ideally suited to Rosenberg, who handles all animals with equal aplomb. Oddly, the perils of pet sitting are not what you'd think. Rosenberg has never been attacked by a dog on the job (though she once had to subdue a dog on the street by punching it in the jaw). She is, however, always on guard against attack cats. "They can jump at you from any angle," she reports. "I never visit a cat without a briefcase for protection."

'TIS THE SEASON

SNOWPLOWING SERVICE

Business:

Clearing driveways and yards of snow

Basic Equipment and Expenses:

$5,000

Necessities:

Vehicle appropriate for plowing (pickup truck, four-wheel drive), flyers, telephone

Experience Required:

None

Inside Tip:

This business can be started for less than $10,000 if you already own a vehicle. A good plow can be bought for less than $4,000, and the additional advertising and administrative costs are minimal. If you have to buy a vehicle as well, add that cost onto the $5,000 estimated above.

Put your truck to work plowing snow for shovel-shy locals. With a relatively inexpensive snowplow attachment, you can turn your regular vehicle into a money-making machine.

Marblehead, Massachusetts, entrepreneur George A. Forbes ran a snowplowing service from his regular business, Forbes Service Station (currently owned by John and Richard Jackson). "I thought it would be a great way to supplement my income," says Forbes. "I already had the equipment [vehicles], and I was looking for a way to maximize their use." Forbes put plows on the front of his trucks, distributed flyers to local mailboxes, and considered himself in business.

Establishing a regular clientele took some time, Forbes reports. "We encouraged people who were especially good customers to give us all their business, including the snowplowing," he says. "Then, it seems like the bigger the storms, the better the business. It's like when you go out to paint a house: All the neighbors come by and ask for an estimate. If you're out plowing someone's yard, someone else will come over and ask you to plow theirs." In time, Forbes's client list grew to include ninety regular accounts.

Perhaps the greatest trick to running a successful snowplowing service is timing. Working people need their driveways plowed by seven A.M. That means, as Forbes points out, "If it starts to snow at seven P.M., you can't start plowing at six A.M." Simplicity is a key factor. Forbes recommends establishing regular accounts—people who pay for your services on a monthly or seasonal basis instead of calling you for each individual job. He also suggests setting up regular routes to minimize travel time. Yet even with the best planning, odd hours are sometimes unavoidable. "You have to provide good service to be successful," Forbes says, "even if that means going out in the middle of the night."

On the other hand, there's time for rest on the off-season. According to Forbes, a typical season in Marblehead lasts from Thanksgiving to mid-April. "After that," he says, "you can start thinking about where you're taking your vacation."

CHRISTMAS-TREE LOT

Business:

Selling Christmas trees from parking lots or empty lots

Basic Equipment and Expenses:

$10,000

Necessities:

Location, cashbox, trees; fence, lights, and trailer may be rented, or provided by your lessor

Experience Required:

None

Inside Tip:

If you find a good location, consider selling other seasonal items like Halloween pumpkins or spring bedding flowers.

You can't grow money on trees, but you can make money selling them. A Christmas-tree lot will do more than raise your holiday spirits. Some operators make enough money in December to last the whole year. Others add a healthy supplement to their regular income, or combine Christmas tree sales with other seasonal businesses to make year-round profits.

Denver, Colorado, entrepreneur George Sato started selling Christmas trees over twenty years ago. A former chick-sexer by trade (he sorted chicks by sex for poultry companies), Sato got into the business because he wanted "something to do" during the winter off-season. Today, Sato's Christmas Trees has become a regular local fixture, with a loyal following that returns from year to year.

Sato observes that the market for independent tree lots has shifted in the past few years. "Big outfits [like supermarkets and hardware chains] sell their trees at cost," he says. With competition like that, low-end business is harder to come by, so Sato focuses on the upscale. "The lot is in a nice area, so I cater to rich people," he reports. "I carry a lot of big trees, the kind of big, quality trees that big stores don't carry."

In peak seasons, Sato has sold as many as 6,000 trees. These days, he's scaled down to between 2,000 and 3,000, with a greater emphasis on quality. Each year, he sells out. The trees he stocks come from farms in Oregon, Washington, Idaho, and California. "Wild trees don't have a good shape," he explains. If at all possible, Sato recommends trying to negotiate credit from tree suppliers. Doing so will reduce your initial start-up costs dramatically.

Since he retired from his job eight or nine years ago, Sato has spent his summers selling bedding plants from the same location. "We're open for about three months," he says. "We have six or seven people to help run the place. I do all the buying and my son Donny handles the cash register. We buy a lot and we sell a lot." In between stands, Sato travels the country visiting his children and grandchildren, enjoying a nice balance between retirement and entrepreneurship.

LIGHTING STRIKES

How Christmas-light king Arnold Mahler turned a simple idea into a national franchise.

"I did not invent Christmas lighting," says Arnold Mahler. "All I did was market it properly."

From Mahler, this is an understatement. In 1986 the lightbulb went on for this ex-retiree. "I hurt my back playing tennis," he explains, "so I hired a local kid to put up my Christmas lights." When neighbors started inquiring about similar services, Mahler saw an opportunity unfolding. He invested about $30,000 in lights, equipment, and help ("I overcapitalized," he believes now), and launched what is currently a nationwide network of lighting technicians.

The Dekra-Lite concept is simple. For an average price of $350, the company will light up a house for the holidays. That price includes design, installation, and removal of the lights. Dekra-Lite also handles commercial accounts—an outgrowth, Mahler says, of the residential business. "The people who owned the homes I was working on also owned commercial buildings," he explains. The following year, they asked him to handle commercial work as well. Today, Mahler's prototype business brings in $250,000 in gross sales for net profits of $85,000—a sizable haul for less than three month's work.

Mahler estimates bare-bones start-up costs for equipment and supplies to be about $7,500 for a new firm (Dekra-Lite franchisees also pay about $8,500 in franchise fees). In addition to marketing materials, ladders, nails, and glue guns, you need lights. But Mahler points out that you can buy those lights as needed with money collected from deposits. "You never have to end up with a negative cash flow in this business," he contends.

Yet if the business is successful, it's primarily due to Mahler's shrewdness. His idea is easy enough to duplicate—

you needn't be a Wharton School graduate to hang Christmas lights. But Mahler's business savvy is more difficult to match. He's a firm believer in thinking big. "You need to look at the forest," he argues, "not the trees. You can't get bogged down with details. You have to know that if three bulbs are out on a string of lights, you don't spend an hour fixing it— you get a new one. You have to work smart, not hard." Mahler believes it's this kind of thinking that's enabled him to make a lucrative venture out of what used to be a part-time, low-profit business.

In the future, Mahler plans to keep expanding the Dekra-Lite franchise network. He's added a new idea to the concept: selling and installing low-voltage landscape lighting. "A lot of my franchisees wanted something to do in the off-season," he says. Personally, Mahler has more than enough work perfecting the Dekra-Lite system and dreaming up new ideas. After all, there are plenty of things he didn't invent that need proper marketing.

12

TAKING CARE

CHILD-CARE REFERRAL AND CONSULTING

Business:

Helping corporate clients set up child-care programs, both on-site and through independent operators

Basic Equipment and Expenses:

$10,000

Necessities:

Computer with database program, telephone, stationery

Experience Required:

Expertise in child care, education, and/or early childhood development necessary

Inside Tip:

Be as diverse as possible to help the widest range of people. Some areas to consider researching: after-school programs, in-home child care, senior day care.

As working moms make up more and more of the American work force, the need for reliable child care is becoming more than a family issue—it's also a business concern. And companies are recognizing that fact. Whether through on-site child care or simple referral services, employers are increasingly eager to lend a hand. The reasoning is not completely altruistic, of course:

Child-care problems can lead to absenteeism or even to an employee's leaving the company.

Yet, most corporations know nothing about child care. They need the services of outside experts like Waltham, Massachusetts, entrepreneur Eleanor Nelson. Her company, Workplace Connections, helps corporate employees locate reliable day care, conducts parenting seminars, and helps companies set up their own on-site child-care centers.

Nelson, a twenty-five-year veteran of the education field, originally got into the business as an on-site child-care consultant. Tenants in a local office park wanted to set up a day-care center, and asked Nelson for her help. But she soon realized that the needs of both employees and employers were extremely diverse. "Small- to medium-sized companies need a broader range of services," she explains. "Just providing on-site day care wasn't going to meet their needs." Many small firms couldn't afford to set up their own centers. And parents expressed a variety of concerns—for instance, many had school-age children who didn't need full-time supervision, just something to do after school.

Nelson's consulting and referral services have become so successful that she has been able to branch out into running her own day-care centers. "We did consultation without operation," she says, "but many developers and corporations didn't want to run the centers themselves. They didn't have the staff, and they wanted to distance themselves from the

operations. After all, they're not in the child-care business."
Opening day-care centers isn't an inexpensive proposition.
Nelson estimates that a small center costs $250,000 to
launch. Client companies are willing to help financially, but
they usually don't cover all the costs. For shoestring operators, actually starting and operating centers would be
strictly a down-the-road move.

Meanwhile, though, the need for quality child care shows
no sign of waning. "The market is there," says Nelson. "It
isn't going to go away. We are very concerned about the
middle-income family. In Massachusetts, parents spend an
average of $5,000 to $10,000 a year for child care. That
creates quite a dilemma for most working people."

INNSITTING SERVICE

Business:

Minding the inn while the innkeepers are away

Basic Equipment and Expenses:

$3,000

Necessities:

Telephone, answering service, business cards

Experience Required:

Innkeeping experience preferred

Inside Tip:

If you've never owned an inn and have no hopes of doing so in
the near future, consider getting a job as an inn manager, or
in some other aspect of the hospitality field.

Everyone's heard of babysitting, housesitting, condo-sitting, and even boat-sitting—but innsitting? Yes, bed-and-breakfast owners who want to take a vacation without losing two weeks' business are turning to innsitters like Annette King of Innsitting Services in Raleigh, North Carolina. As a "roving innkeeper," King has her own business and an opportunity to travel the country to boot.

Before taking the helm at an inn, King expects innkeepers to pay her expenses for two to three days while she learns their way of doing things. Of course, even with this kind of preparation, things sometimes manage to go wrong. In more than three years of innsitting, King has had to deal with the likes of sleepwalkers venturing into her room, hotwater heaters going on the clink, and air conditioners dripping into guests' rooms. "If anything is going to go wrong, it happens as soon as I get there," she kids.

While some innsitters might panic and phone the owners (or just let things go), King handles every crisis in her stride. It's this conscientious attitude that's earned her a five-star rating from innkeepers.

Once King has worked with an inn, she enters everything she's learned about it in her "Innsitting Bible," which is never far from her reach. That way, the next time she sits at the same inn, she'll have her notes on the problems she encountered, and the way things should be done.

One of only a handful of innsitters nationwide, King plans to help others start their own innsitting services by conducting seminars. By her account, innsitting is an agreeable way to do business. "I really like meeting all the new people, and I enjoy traveling," King says. "What I really like best, though, is cooking breakfast. I can cook breakfast for a month and never repeat a single item."

HOUSEHOLD PLACEMENT SERVICE

Business:

Placing child care, elderly care, nursing, pet care, shopping, and personal services professionals in temporary and permanent positions

Basic Equipment and Expenses:

$5,000

Necessities:

Telephone, basic office equipment, insurance, advertising. In some states, a license is required to run a placement agency.

Experience Required:

Some knowledge of the personnel placement business desirable; interviewing skills are important and, on the other side of the business, so is marketing ability

Inside Tip:

Once you've nailed down the basics of placement and management, you can expand your services into other fields. Household placement pro Ilene Nordle began Elite Personnel, a corporate placement firm, as an outgrowth of her original Sitting & Home Care Services.

Over the past decade or so, temporary personnel services have become the darling of the American workplace. Just make a phone call, and a reliable, competent worker will show up at your office ready to do the job. For busy executives, temporary help is an essential convenience.

So is it any wonder that the same busy executives want a similar service when they need someone to care for their children, their elderly relatives, or even their dogs?

Ilene Nordle, founder of Sitting & Home Care Services, Inc. in Fairfield, Connecticut, doesn't think so. Nordle started her household placement/personal services agency from home in 1984 with an initial investment of only $3,000. Nordle links clients with child-care workers, companions for the elderly, nurses, pet sitters, personal shoppers, chauffeurs, and other home-service professionals. All "employees" are independent contractors, which saves Sitting the paperwork and liability costs associated with a large staff. For permanent placements, Nordle charges a flat fee. If an assignment is temporary, she splits a set hourly wage with her workers.

Roughly 450 clients contact Nordle each year for household help. One secret to her success is an impeccable reputation. "We begin by sending out a lengthy application to each client," she says. "Then we look for the right person for the job. When hiring, we're not looking for the average person; we're looking for the excellent person. All our applicants are fingerprinted and all references checked." Apparently, the formula works: Sitting became so big a few years back that Nordle was forced to move her offices from home to a commercial space.

Nordle also consults with people interested in duplicating Sitting's success. "I enjoy working with new business owners," Nordle says. "It gives me some variety. One thing I always emphasize to would-be entrepreneurs is that it takes a lot of time and energy to start a new venture."

HOUSESITTING

Business:

Maintaining people's homes while they're away on vacations

Basic Equipment and Expenses:

$5,000

Necessities:

Telephone, transportation, advertising; home computer recommended

Experience Required:

None, but organization is a must

Inside Tip:

Establish a manageable area that you'd like to work within and stick to it. Driving all over the county will wear you out and cut into your profits.

Returning from a fabulous vacation to dead plants, starving goldfish, a mildewed refrigerator, and a pile of newspapers is anticlimactic, to say the least. And that's not the worst of it. Vacant, untended homes invite burglaries. And what about coffeemaker anxiety—that nagging feeling that you forgot to turn off the coffee?

Every year, these exact scenarios prompt vacationers to hire professional housesitters. Most homes don't require a lot of tending while their owners are gone—but they usually require some. Plants and gardens need watering, mail and newspapers must be collected. Sundry duties abound, like letting in the cleaning service or putting out the trash. If pets are involved, daily or twice-daily visits from a sitter are in order. Yet none of these tasks equals the peace of mind that a sitter can offer anxious travelers. While they're away, they know someone is watching their homes.

Jo Ann Knappenberger is a Torrance, California-based housesitter who's been in business since 1988. Knappenberger's firm, Sitting Pretty, provides twice-daily pet care, occasional home visits, and overnight service to vacationing local residents. Knappenberger combines her basic skills in running a home with some mean organizational talents. A former executive secretary, she brings a high level of professionalism to her business.

"I used to set up offices from scratch," says Knappenberger, "so I knew how it was done." Right off, she computerized her files and accounts, lined up ads in the Yellow Pages, worked out routes, and set up a detailed system of paperwork. She also developed a process for getting acquainted with clients. "As nervous as they might be letting a stranger into their homes, I'm just as worried that they're legitimate," she says. "I do a full interview with clients, so that we're both comfortable with each other."

Knappenberger estimates that she spent $5,000 setting up her business. But in six months she broke even. And shortly thereafter, she began turning a profit. Sitting Pretty charges anywhere from $10 on up per visit, depending on the location and how many pets (if any) are involved. Overnight stays start at $20.

At first, Knappenberger did much of the sitting herself—quite an awakening after working for years in a corporate environment. "When I first started going to houses, I got very depressed," she says. "I thought, 'I was making $35,000 a year and now I'm picking up dog poop. This is kind of a comedown.'" But soon, she realized that her new work offered rewards of its own—not the least of which was "wonderful hugs" from the pets she visited. "They're nicer to me than my daughters," she jokes. Since then, she's also hired help, so she has more time to develop the administrative end of the business.

According to Knappenberger, the market for housesitters is just beginning to be tapped. "Already I've had two offers from people who want to see businesses like this in their own areas," she says. "One man from Tennessee offered to put up $5,000 to put someone in business, if I would screen them and train them." Knappenberger is thinking about consulting, as well as pursuing some interesting new ideas in her own business. One is to run errands for clients while they're away. Working from a list of "twenty-five things that

can be done while someone's on vacation," she may start
providing services like taking electric blankets to the cleaners or organizing linen closets—all in conjunction with her
housesitting.

KEEPING HOUSE

> Brian Graves's temporary home caretaking offers a win-win-win
> situation—for property owners, renters, and Graves himself.

To start a business in the midst of a recession, you need a
pretty good idea. Brian Graves, a Seattle-area real-estate
agent in the early eighties, had one. As the real-estate market
slowed, Graves realized that more and more houses were
sitting vacant. In the real-estate business, it's widely ac-
knowledged that occupied homes are more inviting than
vacant ones. A vacant house feels empty to prospective
buyers. And what's more, a vacant property can cost money.
There's always the threat of vandalism or damage from un-
discovered frozen pipes or leaky roofs—damage that may not
be covered under a homeowner's policy if it has a vacancy
clause.

Recognizing all the problems that vacant properties could
pose—and the fact that many young couples would gladly
look after a vacant house in exchange for lower rent—Graves
launched his Redmond, Washington, firm, America's Home
Caretakers. In truth, Graves had a little help with the concept. Some friends had already worked out arrangements to
sleep over in vacant properties and keep the vandals out. "All
they were doing was staying there," he explains. "They had
card tables and sleeping bags, and they kind of camped out.
But that didn't do anything to enhance the marketing of the
property."

Graves made the concept more marketable. Graves's caretakers bring in attractive furnishings, maintain the yard,
perform minor repairs, and keep the houses immaculate.

They also agree to vacate the property once it's sold. In exchange, they don't pay any rent—just a modest monthly placement fee to Graves. "They're not renters," Graves stresses. "They're there to take care of the house."

Graves markets his service to real-estate companies, financial institutions, and private sellers—virtually anyone with a vacant property is a potential client. At any given time, he has 50 to 100 caretakers placed in local homes. A typical monthly fee for these placements is $150. Though his standards are high, Graves reports no problem recruiting caretakers. Churches and community groups are a good source. At other times, he will visit local real-estate offices. "I stand up and say, 'Would anyone here like to live rent-free for a year and save enough money for a down payment?'" he says. "Just about every hand goes up."

The caretakers concept has been so successful for Graves that he'd like to franchise it eventually. "We're still a young company," he says, "and we don't feel we're ready for that. Our big dream is to franchise. When we do it, we'll do it right." Meanwhile, he has expanded his firm's services to include refurbishing and repairs, as well as real-estate sales.

Starting a temporary caretaking service isn't an expensive proposition, according to Graves. "For just $2,000 to get the licenses and your logo and letterhead, you can be in business," he says. "And you can start this business part-time." But he emphasizes that this isn't a get-rich-quick scheme. Plenty of work is involved. "When we first started [in 1984], some people thought the idea was so simple that they could make some fast money," he says. "It's not that way in this business. You should realize that it takes a lot of hard work."

13

FOR GREEN THUMBS ONLY

LAWN CARE SERVICE

Business:

Mowing, watering, fertilizing, reseeding, and generally maintaining residential and commercial lawns

Basic Equipment and Expenses:

$3,000

Necessities:

Lawn mower, basic gardening/lawn care supplies, transportation

Experience Required:

None, but if your own lawn is brown and weedy, you aren't a good candidate for this business

Inside Tip:

Although working couples and older adults will make up most of your potential market, consider contacting landlord associations in your area. Many landlords prefer to hire professional lawn services: They don't trust tenants to maintain the lawns themselves.

There's a lot more to good lawn care than simple mowing. Watering, fertilizing, weeding, reseeding, and even replacing lawns are as critical to a full-service operation as keeping the grass cut and free of debris.

With so many couples working full-time, what was once considered "weekend work" is now looking more like a job for someone—anyone—else. The growth of the lawn care industry illustrates this trend. According to the Lawn Institute, lawn care services bring in $25 million annually. The Professional Lawn Care Association estimates that the industry is expanding at about 15 to 20 percent per year—and dual-income couples are a big reason why. Harold Floyd of the Old Timers Lawn Service in Indianapolis, Indiana, reports that his traditionally older clientele is getting younger every day. While his customers are still "primarily over 55" (a demographic group that also carries a lot of consumer clout), more and more young professionals are relying on his service.

You may already own most of the equipment you'll need to get started in this business: a lawnmower, basic gardening tools, and a good car or truck. In addition, you'll want a supply of fertilizer and grass seed. Working from home is a smart option, since all of your work will take place on the clients' premises. Besides, as Floyd points out, "We live right in the center of the people we want to attract as customers. Why get an office somewhere else?"

HERB FARMING

Business:

Growing and selling herbs to consumers, restaurants, food manufacturers, cosmetic companies

Basic Equipment and Expenses:

$10,000

Necessities:

Land (farmland is desirable, but a large backyard will do to start), seed, fertilizer, basic gardening tools and supplies

Experience Required:

None, although a green thumb certainly helps

Inside Tip:

Be prepared to work seven days a week. Live plants, unlike most inventory, will not sit unattended for days at a stretch. Even if you're only a part-time operator, your crops—and not your whims—will dictate your hours.

A few years back, the American public didn't know its marjoram from its oregano. But, according to the growing number of herb farmers in America, those days are long gone. Americans are rediscovering the value of a good herb, whether for cooking, landscaping, crafts, cosmetics, or health.

"There are so many ways you can go with herbs," says Sequim, Washington, herb farmer Toni Anderson. "We started out working with culinary herbs and we've pretty much stayed with that. But we have a friend who's a naturopath—she's into medicinal herbs—and that's a whole other field we could get into. We haven't because we don't know much about it, but it's there."

Toni and her husband Terry own Cedarbrook Herb Farm, which was founded twenty-two years ago by Toni's mother. The Andersons devote roughly two acres of their twelve-acre farm to growing herbs and garlic. "The bulk of our business is selling the plants themselves," Toni reports. They also sell specialty vinegars, herbal hot pads, dried cooking herbs, wreaths, and dried flower arrangements from a converted barn. They do a brisk mail-order business. And, in the future, Toni hopes to sponsor cooking and crafts classes for local herb enthusiasts.

Business at Cedarbrook Farm is growing by about one-third every year. "Herbs keep getting more and more popular," Toni says. "People want to find out more about them."

And if the retail herb market is blossoming, so is herbal wholesaling. Restaurants are one source of wholesale business: Many upscale eateries prefer fresh herbs to conventional dried. Cosmetic, perfume, and pharmaceutical companies also represent a potential market, as do herbal tea manufacturers.

The biggest challenge in herb farming, according to Toni Anderson, is keeping up with your market. "I'm always trying to find out what people want, and I'm always trying to offer something new," she says. It's also important to plan ahead. As with any farming venture, the whims of nature can play a significant role in an herb-farming business. A prolonged winter, drought, or the mere change of seasons can dictate your growing, harvesting, and selling patterns. Be prepared for seasonal speed-ups and slumps—they're a built-in part of this business.

To find out more about growing herbs, Toni recommends reading as many books about herbs and gardening as you can. Also, consult your local nursery for area-specific growing tips. "Herbs are fairly easy to grow," says Toni. "I learned the most by being in the business, by just getting out and doing it."

PLANT DESIGN AND MAINTENANCE

Business:

Furnishing businesses and homes with houseplants; following up with weekly maintenance

Basic Equipment and Expenses:

$3,000

Necessities:

Transportation, telephone, watering can, scissors, fertilizer

Experience Required:

None, but the more you know about plants, design, and marketing, the better

Inside Tip:

Consider taking on a partner with complementary skills. Plant service professional Lori Johnson and former partner Christi Chung learned from each other to start.

Los Angeles plant specialist Lori Johnson started her six-year-old firm, Plant Management, with only a modest capital outlay: "I had a two-gallon bucket for water, and I spent $2.69 on a bottle of fertilizer and $12.95 for a good pair of scissors," she says. The rest was all salesmanship, diligence, and a little imagination.

The plant design and maintenance business has grown in popularity over the past decade for several reasons. First, just about everyone agrees that healthy, attractive plants add to the ambience of a home, office, shop, or restaurant. Yet it's difficult for someone who knows nothing about plants to choose the right greenery for the given environment. Is it too hot for a fern? Too bright for a palm? And how does the plant coordinate with the decor? Finally, many people have neither the time nor the expertise to keep their plants in top physical condition.

"We're providing a service for people who just don't have the time to do it themselves," Johnson explains. "They want a service that they don't have to worry about, one that will make them happy."

Johnson started the business in 1983 with former partner Christi Chung, who was studying landscaping at a local community college (Chung has since left the business to raise a family and focus on landscaping). Johnson had worked herself out of a job renting office space to new tenants. "My boss told me I was so good in sales that I should be making money for myself," she recalls. "I didn't appreciate it at the time, but he turned out to be right." With Johnson's sales skills and Chung's green thumb, the partners figured they couldn't go wrong. "We each had talents that the other was lacking," Johnson says. "That's one reason our partnership worked."

Building the new business wasn't easy, though. "We went door to door looking for clients, and we only got five or six," Johnson recalls. To speed the process, the partners decided to buy out an established plant service. With a $1,000 investment from each, they took over Plant Management—and the business has made money ever since.

Today, Johnson has as much business as she can handle working part-time from her home (playwriting and her son Sam take up the rest of her work week). Most of her accounts are businesses, though she does do a few residences, including the home of talk-show host Tom Snyder. "It's a lot easier to go office to office than it is to approach people's homes," she says. "If you present yourself properly and you're offering a real service, businesses will talk to you." Making contacts with contractors and developers will pay off for new plant services, she says, as will good relationships with quality nurseries.

In this business, having a way with both plants and people is the key to success. While it's possible to start out with very little equipment and no outside location (like Johnson), it's not advisable to start out with no skills or marketing plan. "This isn't a business where you can make a lot of money right away," says Johnson. "But you can make nice money if you're good at it and you have a sense of responsibility about what you're doing."

COMING UP POSIES

> Shirley Skinner's gardening business is blooming. "If I got one job a month in the beginning, I was thrilled," she says. "Now, I have a job every day."

Shirley Skinner had a penchant for planting, but no plot to speak of. Alas, her yard was woefully small. "You can only replant the same patch so many times before it wears out," she says. So she found herself at friends' and relatives' houses digging up weeds and putting in petunias. Finally a friend suggested that she do this for a living. But Skinner wasn't sure there was a market for her particular talents.

"There were gardeners," she says, "but around here all they want to do is mow, blow, and go. Then there were landscapers, but they put on a big production." Skinner wasn't as expedient as the typical gardener, but she wasn't as erudite as a landscape architect. Was there really room for her in the garden?

The argument, as Skinner recalls it, went something like this: "My friend said, 'Look, you can help housewives with their snapdragons. I put in snapdragons every year and they don't bloom. Do you know why?' I said, 'Yeah, you don't give them enough sun.' And she said, 'See! You can help people.'" With $130, Skinner got some business cards and a few T-shirts and started moonlighting. A month later, she was convinced that her South Pasadena, California, business, The Posie Pushers, could fly.

Skinner specializes in rehabilitating older gardens. While most landscapers prefer to start anew with projects, she weeds out the dead wood, transplants anything that looks out of place, puts in new perennials and annuals, and brings the garden back to life. "Most of my clients have older homes," she explains. "Most of my work is bringing back gardens that have been let go. Then we provide monthly maintenance—deadheading, weeding, trimming, cultivating, fertilizing, and treating for snails. I still don't have any competition in what I'm doing," she continues, "I suspect it's too much work for most people."

In truth, it's sometimes too much for Skinner as well. She has three full-time associates and still works long hours designing new gardens, drawing up proposals, and actually working in the yards. She's up at seven A.M. loading the vans for the day, and home about six P.M. to do the unloading. "I'm the one that's holding the company back," she confesses. "It's hard to find enough hours in the day."

This wouldn't be a problem if Skinner didn't have a natural talent for getting herself noticed. Her first "sample garden" was at a commercial building. She offered to install and maintain a garden for free in exchange for a small sign promoting The Posie Pushers. "That helped, because when I'd talk to clients, they'd ask if I had any gardens they could see," Skinner explains. "I'd send them to that building."

When a new landlord came in and canceled the agreement, Skinner worked out a similar arrangement at the local post office. "I spent about $1,200 out of pocket in labor and plants for that garden," says Skinner, "but it was the biggest brainstorm I ever had in my life." Not only did Skinner get tremendous exposure ("Talk about foot traffic!" she raves), but she also got several awards. "When I went to get the L.A. Beautiful Award, the program had listed all the people who won," Skinner recalls. "And under 'gardens' they had 'So-and-so, landscape architect' and all these names of design firms. Next to the post office, it said 'The Posie Pushers.'

What a laugh." Apparently, she was more professional than she thought.

Yet she hasn't lost the original spark that got her into the business to start. Wherever she goes, she's constantly on the lookout for new gardening ideas. And she hasn't lost her feel for the soil and for planting, either. "This work is great because you can stand up and see what you've done," she says. "It's instant gratification."

14

THE TOURIST TRADE

COLLEGE CAMPUS TOURS

Business:

Escorting college-bound high school students to various college campuses

Basic Equipment and Expenses:

$10,000

Necessities:

Telephone, brochures. Marketing, legal, and insurance expenses can be relatively substantial

Experience Required:

Familiarity with college campuses and programs a must. Ability to work well with teenagers and help guide them through the evaluation process is also important

Inside Tip:

Don't overestimate your salesmanship. "On our first tour, we booked a bus for 40 people," recalls tour operator Margy Arthur. "Two students showed up. It was very humbling. It's important to be realistic."

Too many of us chose our colleges for all the wrong reasons. We went for the school with the nicest brochure. Or we looked for the most favorable male-female ratio. We might as well have drawn names from a hat. But then, what choices did we have? For students living on the West Coast, for example, Eastern colleges like Haverford and Bard are virtually unheard of. And without seeing the various campuses in person, who can make a rational decision?

Count Margy Arthur among those people whose college choice was less than scientific. Her parents moved to Japan just before she went off to school, so she picked a college close to the Orient: UCLA. Though she has no regrets, Arthur is set on changing the way high-school students choose their colleges. Her Pleasanton, California, company, College Campus Tours, escorts groups of college-bound seniors and juniors on tours of East coast, Southern California, and Northwestern campuses.

"The tours are very structured and very fast-paced," says Arthur. "But in a matter of three or four days, they become so sophisticated. Once they've been on a tour, they often can go visit additional campuses by themselves [and know what to look for]."

As a guide, Arthur provides students with a view of college life they wouldn't get on their own. "One of the things I do is sit everyone down and tell them to watch for a student who looks dynamic, like someone they'd like to show them around," she says. "Then I'll offer that person $10 or so to give us a tour. College students are always looking for money. And they're able to tell the kids what they really want to know about a school. At first, the kids on the tour are so embarrassed. But then they see that it's sometimes the best way to get a tour."

To round out the tour experience, she encourages eating in the dining halls. She arranges one night's stay on campus on every tour, so students can try out dorm life. On the bus between stops, students fill out evaluation forms for each college, so they'll be able to sort through all the information once they return home. Arthur brings an educational guidance counselor along on each tour to help students fill in the informational gaps.

The price for a four-day tour of the East coast is $1,500; eight-day tours cost $1,800. Most of Arthur's business comes from referrals from independent educational counselors and high-school administrators. While Arthur has been successful in keeping the service growing, she notes that marketing has been her biggest expense—and biggest challenge. Simply getting the word out takes a lot of time and money. Insurance has also been a hurdle: Arthur eventually had to call her state government for help finding an insurance company.

Arthur stresses that tour groups must be relatively large in order to be profitable. Officially, she requires a minimum of six students on every tour. (At times she's escorted as few as two students. "I don't make money," she reasons, "but it's been enjoyable.") Business skills have been the most difficult for Arthur to master. Originally, she had two partners who handled much of the accounting and marketing. Now, she's learning these processes herself.

Arthur identifies her main strengths in this business as organization, strong nerves, and a genuine interest in teens. "I enjoy working with students of all ages," she says. "They really grow on these tours, they learn a lot."

BICYCLE TOURING

Business:

Hosting bicycle tours of the local sights or foreign countries

Basic Equipment and Expenses:

$10,000

Necessities:

Telephone, marketing brochures. Cycling gear and equipment for yourself, helmets for all. The following should be on hand, but may be rented depending on the situation: van for carrying tired tourists and gear, bicycles for tourists who have none

Experience Required:

Cycling and traveling experience (unless you hire people to conduct the tours, thereby eliminating the fun for you); marketing know-how a plus

Inside Tip:

Get some experience (and some potential referrals) by volunteering to guide church or school groups on local trips.

Many business owners don't get vacations for years after start-up. In the bicycle touring business, you'll be taking vacations almost immediately. Bicycle tours are gaining in popularity—and with good reason. Bike-riding gives travelers an ideal perspective on an area. The pace is leisurely, the riding is run, and, of course, all that exercise enables vacationers to eat without a guilty conscience.

When Berkeley, California, entrepreneur Tom Hale started Backroads Bicycle Tours in 1979, he had never heard of the bicycle touring business. But, in Hale's words, "I wanted to do something active, something outdoors." After ten months as an environmental planner, he quit his job and set out on a five-thousand-mile bike trip. When he returned, he determined to start a bicycle touring business of his own.

Ten years later, Hale's company bills itself as North America's premier bicycle touring company. In 1988, Backroads accompanied over 6,000 passengers on tours worldwide for gross sales of over $4 million. According to Hale, these tours are not for wilderness buffs only. "Our focus is vacationing," he says. "It just happens to be vacationing on a bicycle." To underscore that idea, Backroads offers clients a host of creature comforts, including gourmet lunches, deluxe accommodations, quality equipment rentals, and customized vans and trailers to cater to all their clients' whims.

Of course, it wasn't always so. Hale remembers the days when guests ate cake out of cups. Backroads grew into a first-rate organization one step at a time, through years of experience and careful evaluation. Finding new routes that are accessible to a wide range of cyclists is one ongoing challenge. Another is planning an annual itinerary that keeps Hale's staff employed year-round (trips to Baja California, Hawaii, and Australia help take the bite out of winter).

Starting a bicycle touring business for $10,000 or less in the current market will take some serious cost-cutting and strategic planning. And since limited funds may also limit the number of trips you can take at first, keeping a regular job while the business gets off the ground is practically a must. "It's more difficult to enter and succeed in this market right now because the adventure travel industry has evolved some very sophisticated literature and marketing," says Hale. "If I were to recommend someone start up a new business with certainty of success, I'd recommend they go into laundromats."

Still, few other businesses combine work with play more effectively. Hale hasn't taken a vacation in years. Then again, when going to work means touring China and the châteaux of France, who needs time off?

BED AND BREAKFAST RESERVATION SERVICE

Business:

Reserving rooms for guests at local bed and breakfast places

Basic Equipment and Expenses:

$10,000

Necessities:

Telephone, advertising; typewriter and/or personal computer recommended

Experience Required:

Must like people and be a keen judge of character

Inside Tip:

Assess the need for a B&B reservation service in your area. Three questions to answer: What is the tourism potential in my area? Does this service already exist? What can I provide that traditional lodgings and B&Bs alone can't?

Get in on America's bed and breakfast trend without converting your house into a showplace of creature comforts. Bed and breakfast reservation services locate homey accommodations for tourists, then collect a commission from the hosts they represent. "I'm really an agent," says Cambridge, Massachusetts, entrepreneur Pamela Carruthers, owner of Bed and Breakfast. "I work for my hosts."

During the past decade or so, bed and breakfast places have become a popular alternative to traditional lodging. And no wonder: For weary travelers, B&Bs add new meaning to the term "home away from home." Country inns pride themselves on hospitality, down-home charm, and home-cooked breakfasts. And in large cities, where rooms can cost upwards of $200 per night, B&Bs provide an inexpensive alternative to the plush but impersonal service of hotels.

Starting a B&B referral service doesn't require much in the way of equipment. Carruthers says she knows of a successful service owner who doesn't even own a typewriter. Instead, "the telephone becomes your life," Carruthers says. Working from home is especially desirable (standard hours are 8 A.M. to 10 P.M.), so overhead is low.

You do need capital, however, to place ads in B&B guidebooks to reach tourists, and in newspapers and regional magazines to recruit potential hosts. Also, Carruthers notes, you need money to live on while the business takes off—a considerable lag time usually exists from the placement of the first ad until the calls start coming in.

The most important skill for any aspiring B&B reservationist to develop, according to Carruthers, is being able to read people. She cultivates good personal relationships with all her hosts, and takes the time to size up clients so she can make appropriate matches.

"It's important that I have a sense of the customer, because I'm placing them in people's homes," she says. "In cities, where the demand for B&Bs is the greatest, you're often literally renting out a room in someone's house. If I feel there's anything odd about a person, or if someone sounds flaky, I'll tell them there's nothing available."

Carruthers's personal involvement in the business is a limiting factor on growth. "We haven't made any mistakes so far," she says. "There have been no lawsuits, no one's been attacked. An awful lot of that has to do with personal interaction, and how big can you get when you want to maintain that personal interaction?"

On the other hand, it's that personal touch that makes the business enjoyable. "This business gives you a very positive impression of the public," Carruthers says. "The people who stay at bed and breakfasts are usually very nice.

And tourists are a pretty refreshing group—they see everything new and exciting in a city you might have grown bored with."

TOURS FOR SCANDAL

> Rick London's Scandal Tours of Washington show a side of the nation's capital you don't learn about in high school.

It started out as a promotional gimmick. Rick London, a writer for Washington, D.C.'s satirical theater group Gross National Product, wanted to publicize his new production, *Bushcapades*. For $1,800, he hired some actors from the troupe, rented a tour bus, and ran an ad in the *Washington Post*. Scandal Tours of Washington attracted so much interest from people in the tourist trade that London began to rethink his venture.

"I immediately got calls from people who thought we were an established business," London says. "That's what got me thinking that this could be a real business. I went out and had $500 worth of promotional brochures printed up, bought mailing lists, and did some presentations to different hotel associations." The rest, as they say, is history.

Which is fitting, since London is a historian of sorts—not the sort you remember from high-school history class, but a more cynical kind. London's tour highlights some of Washington's humbler monuments: Gary Hart's townhouse, the Watergate building. Even the usual postcard sites have their resident embarrassments, and London reveals them all. Along the way, actors impersonate some of Washington's finest. A Fawn Hall look-alike distributes souvenir shreds of paper. A George Bush impersonator bumbles through his monologue.

Scandal Tours isn't conventional sightseeing, to say the least. But in a city teeming with tours, having a point of departure makes perfect sense. "If you look at regular tours, there are no Yuppie-aged people on them," London points out. "We realized pretty quickly that they were our target market. They aren't our only market—we have eighty-year-olds on our tours all the time—but they're a group that's usually overlooked."

Yuppies aren't the only ones tuned in to London's tours. The media has also jumped on the Scandal bandwagon. With both local and national coverage, London has done a minimum of advertising to get the word out about his new business.

Scandal Tours run seven days a week. On weekends, the tours are open to the public; during the week, tours are specially arranged for travel groups, conventions, and so on. The tours cost $20 per person or $30 with drinks and hors d'oeuvres at the Ritz Carlton to round out the trip. London books an average of two tours a week, though he believes his current promotional efforts will increase that volume substantially. In addition to developing the business locally, London and his partner John Simmons hope to launch their idea in London, England. If that's a hit, they plan to move into other European cities.

Though he admits he's found a "lot to learn" in running this business, London isn't new to entrepreneurship. Between 1979 and 1981, he owned a health-food store. "It was a complete failure, a total flop," he says. "I was young. I had no management skills. I tried to expand before the business was making money." This time around, London is a little wiser. His overhead is low—he works out of his home—and he's focusing his efforts on sales, for which he has a certain knack.

Jokingly, London says, "I wouldn't recommend this business to anyone who wants to maintain his sanity." But seriously, he reports a great deal of interest from the travel industry, associations, international groups, and individual tourists. Tourists are looking for a fresh angle, London says. Incidentally, he's not the only one to offer an offbeat tourist service. A Chicago company conducts tours of famous gangster hangouts; a Los Angeles firm guides people through notorious death sites.

You don't need experience in tourism to succeed in a business like this. But, according to London, you do need a keen imagination. "The long-hour theory is beyond truth," he says. "If there were a time clock, I'd get paid while I'm dreaming."

15

BUSINESS TO BUSINESS

TEMPORARY HELP SERVICE

Business:

Placing workers in various temporary jobs, ranging from clerical work to industrial, management, and professional positions

Basic Equipment and Expenses:

$10,000: an additional line of credit to cover payroll expenses strongly recommended

Necessities:

Office space and furniture, telephone, typewriter, home computer, business stationery

Experience Required:

Experience in the temporary-help industry invaluable; must be a sharp personnel manager as well as a good salesperson

Inside Tip:

Get some experience in the business before you start. Not only will you learn the ins and outs of the business, but you may also spot untapped niches in the market.

All around the country, temporary work is becoming a way of life. Recent college graduates use temporary jobs to familiarize themselves with various companies. Struggling artists may "temp" to meet expenses while their careers take off. People who've recently relocated need work to tide them over until they find permanent employment. And many workers simply enjoy the flexibility of working in the temporary industry. For employers, temps can boost productivity during seasonal rushes, deal with special projects, and take over for sick and vacationing employees.

But perhaps the biggest winner of all is the temporary help service. The temporary help industry is over $5 billion strong—and growing. And considering the growth potential a successful temp service offers, this isn't a particularly expensive business to get into.

Partners Lee Nold and Judy Litteer started ProServ, a San Francisco temporary help service, in 1987 with a small cash investment and a large line of credit. In five months, they broke even. In their first year of business, they grossed over $1 million. "A lot of people think—as I once did—that you need a huge bankroll to meet the payrolls of all these temps," says Nold. "But that wasn't our experience. We didn't even use all of our line of credit."

Nold says that experience made all the difference. "Both my partner and I were very knowledgeable about the industry when we started," she says. "Since we knew what we were doing, we didn't have to work the fourteen and fifteen hour days you hear other people talking about. We were able to work smart, not hard." They did, however work alone. It wasn't until their eleventh month that the partners hired the first employee. "We did everything ourselves," says Nold. "We interviewed every temp; we called every client. We did it all."

Nold stresses that a good temporary help service should do more than just match employees with clients. ProServ offers free computer training to qualified applicants. "Many of our word-processing temps know five or ten software programs," Nold reports. ProServ also provides benefits, holiday and vacation pay, and bonuses for referrals and requests. "Good, skilled people are hard to find," she says. Incentives play an important role in keeping the best temps on the payroll.

And Nold needs as many temps as she can get. Demand for temporary services has done anything but wane. "Companies around here are very sensitive to possible downturns," Nold says. "If they aren't sure a job is going to last for years and years, they'd rather hire a temp than face layoffs." In the future, ProServ will expand into new fields of temporary work, including computer programming, systems analysis, and management. The market is growing, says Nold, and she's eager to grow with it. "I took to this business right away," she says. "It's instant gratification. You know right away where you stand, what you've accomplished."

SECRETARIAL/WORD PROCESSING SERVICE

Business:

Providing all the services a secretary would, but in an independent environment. Typing, transcribing, dictation, editing, and xeroxing are some typical services

Basic Equipment and Expenses:

$10,000

Necessities:

Telephone, typewriter, home computer with laser printer, copier, office supplies

Experience Required:

Good clerical skills a must

Inside Tip:

Develop a specialty. The legal and medical fields are just a few that need particular expertise.

If you're a qualified secretary, you don't have to put up with a miserable boss. In fact, you don't have to tolerate a boss at all. With a modest investment in equipment and supplies, you can take your work home and do it on your own terms.

Don't most offices have their secretarial needs covered? According to those in the field, the answer is no. Many small businesses can't afford to hire secretaries. Other firms, including law offices and medical practices, may have more work than their staffs can handle.

Shelia Young, owner of Young's Secretarial Service in Oakland, California, has so much work that she and her staff are inundated. Sixteen hour days have become almost routine. Young's provides a variety of services: word processing, medical transcription (hard-to-transcribe tapes are a specialty), copying, binding, and editing. Young has special expertise in legal documents, and gets a fair amount of work from public agencies as well as private companies.

Young reports that starting a secretarial service is by no means an invitation to leisure. "About 90 percent of our work is rush work, and we pride ourselves on getting everything out on deadline," Young says. Moreover, flexible hours aren't always an option. "Just because you work for yourself, you can't come in whenever you want," she reports. "You have to be in at nine A.M. every day because your clients expect it."

The skills Young considers most important to her business are management ability and, on the other side of the spectrum, excellent typing and shorthand. She urges would-be owners of secretarial services to make sure they have a strong emotional support network and enough capital to keep them afloat while they're getting their businesses running. "When I went into business [in 1973], it was a lot easier financially than emotionally, because women didn't start businesses," she says. "Now, it's far easier emotionally than financially."

COLLECTION AGENCY

Business:

Collecting money owed on delinquent accounts

Basic Equipment and Expenses:

$3,000

Necessities:

Telephone, answering service, business cards

Experience Required:

Familiarity with the credit industry extremely helpful

Inside Tip:

Take stock of the competition and ask yourself what you can offer that they don't. Finding a competitive edge can help you get your business going.

According to Richard Schultz, founder of the National Revenue Corporation in Columbus, Ohio, collections is a $33 billion industry in America. Of the roughly 6,500 agencies in the U.S., the average number of employees is eleven and only seven are nationwide companies. "It's a cottage industry," says Schultz.

When he started National Revenue in 1973, Schultz was a part of that cottage industry. Working from his home bedroom (and incidentally, it was an apartment, not a house), Schultz laid the foundation for one of the largest and most successful agencies in the history of collections. He didn't start with much: just an answering service. "I thought I'd hit the big time when I could afford to hire a Kelly Girl part-time," he laughs. In a week, his business was in the black. Two years later, at age twenty-four, Schultz put his first million in the bank—and there were more to follow. In 1988, National Revenue served over 25,000 active clients and employed 1,200 people nationwide.

If Schultz's success isn't proof enough that collections can be a lucrative business, consider America's growing dependence on credit. "Five years ago, one dollar out of every five went toward paying off some form of indebtedness," says Schultz. "Today, it's one dollar out of every four. We're a boom-or-bust, recession-proof business." Indeed, when times are bad, people tend to rely on credit, and often can't meet their payments. And when times are good, everywhere you hear the cry, "Charge it!"

Schultz believes that solid management and "hiring the best people" have contributed most to his prosperity. That isn't to say that salesmanship and tenacity aren't important—these are the measures of a good collections agent. But, according to Schultz, continued growth is simpler than that. "You have to provide value," he says. "We pay attention to detail and are committed to excellence. That's what's kept us growing."

To beginners, Schultz suggests starting small and finding an untapped niche. "At first, we contacted doctors and dentists and car dealerships," he says. "It was those smaller accounts that enabled us to progress to the kinds of national accounts we service today."

MEETING PLANNING

Business:

Planning corporate meetings: especially locating sites, negotiating contracts, and lining up services

Basic Equipment and Expenses:

$3,000

Necessities:

Telephone, letterhead, brochure/flyer, advertising

Experience Required:

Familiarity with both corporate meetings and available sites extremely helpful

Inside Tip:

If you enjoy travel, this business has special benefits for you. Visiting potential meeting sites isn't all work—it's all a good excuse for an enjoyable trip.

National corporations hold meetings in every corner of the country, which poses a particular problem for the folks in the home office: If you live and work in Houston, Texas, how do you find a suitable location in Denver? Or Las Vegas? Or Burlington, Vermont?

Calling one of the growing numbers of meeting planners is probably a good start. Meeting planners take the guesswork out of planning a corporate gathering, whether it's a convention for 900 or a seminar for ten. Professional meeting planners provide a range of services. Some offer all-out coordination—from choosing a site to supervising the caterers. Others, like Shirley Marley of The Meeting Specialist in Mission Viejo, California, focus on a single aspect of planning. In Marley's case, it's finding locations.

Marley has experience in both the planning and hospitality fields—first as an employee of a major hotel, then as a meeting planner for a cosmetics company. When she decided to launch her own business, she toured facilities around the country and compiled a list of good locations. Then she wrote to 650 in-house meeting planners to offer her services. Marley's expertise costs clients nothing: She earns a commission from hotels and resorts on the overnight charges. In fact, she often saves clients money by securing the best possible rates from hotels looking for repeat business.

Marley doesn't usually handle any of the food and beverage service or other auxiliary services that go along with a meeting. She simply provides site information and negotiates contracts on her clients' behalf. She doesn't attend meetings, either. "It's usually not necessary," she says.

Because her services are relatively simple, they have to be extraordinary. Personal attention is a must. "I avail myself to clients as early as they want or as late as they want," Marley says. "They'll call me from airports or phone booths. I'll take things right to their houses if they ask me to. It's completely service in this business." Having prime locations is also important, and Marley is always on the lookout. Recently, she planned a houseboat excursion on Lake Tahoe for a group of corporate bigwigs. "People are always looking for something different," she reports.

INFORMATION BROKERING

Business:

Finding and analyzing information for legal, financial, or corporate clients

Basic Equipment and Expenses:

$8,000

Necessities:

Microcomputer, printer, and modem

Experience Required:

Basic research skills are helpful. Familiarity with on-line information services and databases will cut down substantially on cost and learning time

Inside Tip:

Choosing a specialty will increase your chances of success. General information brokers do exist, but specialized brokers usually develop a niche faster.

Since 1980, Research Information Services in Washington, D.C., has been locating government and court documents for legal and financial clients. With very little marketing, the firm has doubled its business every year.

"The people we work for are under a lot of pressure to come through with information," says company vice president Bill O'Neill. "They need to have someone they know without a doubt they can depend on. We have established an excellent reputation for accuracy, dependability, and very rapid turnaround time."

Though most of us don't think of information as a salable commodity, information brokering is a $1.6 billion industry in the United States. Most of that revenue is generated by the industry's twenty largest companies, but smaller firms are springing up everywhere. And many are giving the big guns a run for their money.

Information brokering is a relatively new small-business opportunity. Before the advent of the microcomputer, a small-scale research service would not have been able to retrieve, catalog, store, and sell information to clients in a cost-effective way.

But today, with the help of electronic information services and databases, an information broker can locate all varieties of information efficiently and with remarkable speed. For the millions of small- to mid-size companies out there who need to keep abreast of industry trends and conduct market research without the help of in-house researchers, independent information brokers are a godsend.

What do information brokers do? Typically, they gather information from public libraries and electronic information sources, analyze their findings, and assemble detailed reports.

Within those parameters, a raft of potential specialities exists. Research Information, for example, specializes in government documents. Helen Burwell of Burwell Enterprises in Houston, Texas, deals in legal information. Burwell argues that the specialty you choose is not as important as your marketing strategy and the work you do. Providing personal attention and a rapid turnaround can give smaller firms an edge, even over large competitors.

The basic equipment you'll need to set up shop—a microcomputer, printer, and modem—can be bought for under $3,000. In addition, you will need to subscribe to one or more electronic information services (for a sample list, see the sources below). While the subscription fees shouldn't cost too much, the on-line time you'll spend learning to use them might. Try to establish some familiarity with electronic (and conventional) researching techniques before you launch your business.

Once you've learned the tricks of the information trade, the payoff can be substantial. Our research showed that, after breaking even, one-person info brokers charging $60 per hour can bill from $40,000 to over $100,000 per year.

For More Information:

Association of Independent Information Professionals
P.O. Box 71053
Shorewood, Wisconsin 53211
(713) 537-9051

DIALOG Information Services, Inc.
Marketing Department
3460 Hillview Avenue
Palo Alto, California 94304
(415) 858-2700/(800) 334-2564

CompuServe
5000 Arlington Centre Blvd.
P.O. Box 20212
Columbus, Ohio 43260
(800) 848-8199

Dow/Jones News Retrieval Service
P.O. Box 300
Princeton, New Jersey 08543-0300
(609) 520-4000

VU/TEXT Information Services, Inc.
325 Chestnut Street, Suite 1300
Philadelphia, Pennsylvania 19106
(800) 258-8080

NewsNet
945 Haverford Road
Bryn Mawr, Pennsylvania 19010
(800) 345-1301

BRS Information Technologies
1200 Route 7
Latham, New York 12110
(800) 468-0908

BUSINESS CONSULTING

Business:

Helping companies develop a particular aspect of their operations, including accounting, marketing, planning, efficiency, franchising, customer service, financing, etc.

Basic Equipment and Expenses:

$3,000

Necessities:

Varies with the type of consulting. Telephone, letterhead, basic office equipment are standard; home computer may also be essential

Experience Required:

Must have expertise in a specific area of business

Inside Tip:

Don't rely on advertising to attract clients. "This isn't the kind of business that people shop for in the Yellow Pages," says marketing consultant Joan Schaefer. Person-to-person selling and contacts are the best source of business.

If you have business expertise, you have the basic tools to start a consulting business. Today's companies are under tremendous pressure to compete. Yet most want to keep their operations streamlined. Consultants who specialize in everything from marketing to accounting are in high demand these days—and with good reason. Consultants give companies access to valuable input without the long-term expense of hiring a full-time staff.

Joan Schaefer, a Cleveland, Ohio, marketing consultant, helps small companies map out new sales strategies and revamp their existing marketing programs. Since she started her firm in January, 1989, she's been involved in launching a new video product and preparing a local company for expansion.

A ten-year veteran of corporate marketing, Schaefer got into the consulting business almost by accident. She left her job to work in real estate. On a lark, a local company called to ask for her help in evaluating their customer service. Schaefer took the assignment and ended up with more. Now, she's working sixty hours a week and turning inquiries away.

For the companies that hire her, Schaefer's services are a real boon. They get expertise on an hourly basis without the commitment and paperwork that go along with hiring a full-time employee. And Schaefer benefits too. "For one thing, my hourly rate is much higher than it would be if I were an employee—that's just the way consulting works," she says. "Also, the flexibility is nice. If I need to take time out during the day, I can make up those hours in the evenings or on weekends. My commute is about ten seconds from my kitchen table to my office. And I avoid the politics that go with working for a company."

Schaefer urges aspiring business consultants to prepare themselves for the challenges of running their own firms before getting started. "They should recognize that taking the time to get an education and some experience will pay off in the end," she says. "They should develop good business contacts. And they should be comfortable with their personal financial situations, because in consulting you can work eighty hours one week and then go without work for the next month."

Schaefer also points out that consulting work is different from the typical employee experience. "Consulting is more planning and analyzing and less executing," she says. "You create and plan and sometimes you never get to see the results. Some people don't mind that, but it's good to know that in advance."

COMPUTER CONSULTING

Business:

Helping businesses get the most from their computer hardware and software. May include offering advice on purchasing, creating custom programs, training employees to use the systems, general troubleshooting, and phone consultation

Basic Equipment and Expenses:

$10,000

Necessities:

Most consultants consider owning their own systems compulsory. However, in some settings it's possible to use only your client's equipment. Telephone, transportation, and business cards needed

Experience Required:

Must be computer literate. Many consultants come from backgrounds at computer companies; others develop expertise on one job and carry it over into the next. Strong communications skills are also required

Inside Tip:

Don't neglect your people skills. If you're as incomprehensible as an instruction manual, your services won't be appreciated.

Computers are here to stay. Experts predict that one out of three jobs will require computer literacy by the year 2000. By now, most office workers are familiar with computer basics—word processing, data entry, and so on. But relatively few people can write a program or select the right hardware and software for a specialized task.

That's where computer consultants come in. A consultant can bridge the gap between common rudimentary knowledge and the kind of technical expertise needed to set up a new system—or modify an old one when requirements change.

Kathleen Mattson of KM Consulting in Phoenix has been running a computer-consulting business out of a converted garage since 1988. A self-taught expert in graphics software, Mattson developed her skills while working for General Parametrics Corporation in Berkeley, California. "It got to the point where software users would call the company and ask for me when they needed help," she says. "I realized then that I had the makings of a successful consulting business."

Computer consulting holds plenty of advantages for people with the right combination of skills. If you're good, you can command high pay and flexible hours. And besides, for avowed computer buffs, the work itself is a perk. "I love what I'm doing," says Mattson. "It's both a hobby and a job for me, and I don't even have to leave home to do it!"

SECRET SHOPPER SERVICE

Business:

Monitoring customer service and sales performance for stores, restaurants, car dealerships, hotels, etc.

Basic Equipment and Expenses:

$3,000

Necessities:

Telephone, transportation; home computer is helpful, but not indispensable

Experience Required:

Knowledge of basic selling and customer-service techniques; ability to analyze data gathered during anonymous shopping excursions

Inside Tip:

If you're at a loss for creating your own evaluation system, ask a secret shopper in another area of the country if they'll consult with you. The price you pay for help could save you hours (or months) of research and development—and give your business the credibility of a proven system.

Have you ever been so ignored, insulted, neglected, and mistreated at a store that you thought to yourself "I could teach them a thing or two about customer service"? Perhaps you can. As stores, restaurants, hotels, and other consumer businesses try to beef up their customer service, the demand for "secret shopping" services is on the rise.

What is a secret shopper? A secret shopper goes into a

store posing as a regular customer. He or she then evaluates the store's service, based on prearranged standards of courtesy, promptness, knowledgeability, salesmanship, and so on. The information provided by the shopping service helps management determine its service strengths, as well as areas that call for additional training.

According to Robert Sinclair, president of Sinclair Service Assessments in San Antonio, Texas, retailers can't afford to ignore their front-line service if they hope to stay competitive. "No matter what your business, you probably have competitors who have a certain amount of parity with you," says Sinclair. "They have the same merchandise, the same kind of store—and it's hard to set yourself apart. The one thing that can set you apart is customer service." Yet, says Sinclair, very few companies maintain their own standards. "The intention of top management is to provide good service," he explains, "but they have no way to follow up on their training, to monitor what's really going on."

Sinclair spent a year developing an evaluation system that he believes is unusually accurate, objective, and complete. With the help of industry specialists, he created a data questionnaire that covers both the technical and "personality" aspects of customer service. He's also devised a way to categorize and graph the information he gathers, so that managers can access data at a glance.

Sinclair and his network of some fifty part-time shoppers are targeting large, national chains—they're the firms that can afford his high-quality (and more expensive) services. But starting small and locally is also possible for would-be secret shoppers. As Sinclair points out, overhead is low in this business. And equipment needs are also small: A home computer will help you process information, but is not an absolute necessity to start.

The toughest part of selling secret-shopping services, according to Sinclair, is convincing top management to make room in the budget. Though they almost unanimously agree that these services are valuable, they don't always have the funds to hire you. For firms that do, however, the financial rewards can be substantial. Improved salesmanship almost always translates into improved sales—and more satisfied customers. "It costs five times more to go out and get a new customer than it does to retain one you already have," says Sinclair. "Companies that take care of their customers ultimately spend less on advertising."

RELOCATION SERVICE

Business:

Helping the families of relocated employees adjust to the new move

Basic Equipment and Expenses:

$10,000

Necessities:

Presentable office/conference space for meeting with clients, telephone, marketing materials

Experience Required:

Varies with the kinds of services you provide. At the very least, good communication and marketing skills are essential

Inside Tip:

Don't cut corners on your marketing materials. Since many of your clients will be major corporations, your brochures must reflect a professional corporate image.

"Previously, the assumption was that if an employee was offered a relocation, he or she would take it," says Cleveland entrepreneur Marjorie Shorrock of Resource Careers. "That just isn't true anymore." Apparently, two-income couples are only half as mobile as the old one-income models—and major corporations are waking up to that fact.

One way corporations can help smooth the transition for uprooted families is to offer help. For example, Shorrock and partner Cathy Lewis provide employment services for spouses of relocated employees. "We give them counseling. We provide them with contacts in the job market. We offer information on some of the employers in the area," Shorrock says. "We don't guarantee placement, but we're here to help."

Resource Careers began as a nonprofit group. In 1987, Shorrock and Lewis decided the time was ripe for the venture to turn a profit. The major change in becoming a for-profit organization, according to Shorrock, is the switch in emphasis from a combination of individual counseling and corporate work to just corporate contracts. Most of their client companies are "Fortune 500 companies who, as part of their general management decisions, relocate their employees," says Shorrock. Many are also using Resource Careers' services to entice new employees to join up. Whatever the motives, the concept works. The partners expect their second year's sales to double their first's.

Though Shorrock and Lewis seem rightfully pleased with their focus on spousal employment, other areas can be explored. In our research, we've come across relocation services that help transplanted families find the right neighborhoods, evaluate local school systems, and locate new family doctors, dentists, and so on.

ORGANIZING SERVICE

Business:

Putting homes and offices in order; includes sorting through backed-up paperwork, setting up filing systems, coaching time-management skills, and sundry other organizing tasks

Basic Equipment and Expenses:

$2,500

Necessities:

Telephone, transportation, business cards/stationery

Experience Required:

None, but obviously a knack for organization helps

Inside Tip:

Mind your manner. To sell your skills as an organizer, you have to project an organized image. Professional organizer Marti Snider says, "If you have a run in your stockings, people notice. They watch to see if you have a daily organizer. They'll follow you out to your car to see if it's clean."

Whatever happened to the paperless office? Years ago, we were promised offices so streamlined and so organized that we would never have to wade through paperwork again. Computers, we were told, would handle it all.

Needless to say, it hasn't happened. The average office has stacks, files, boxes, drawers, cartons, and envelopes full of paper. The only difference is that now computer disks are likely to be mixed in with the lot.

"I work with people who haven't opened their mail for a year," says Beverly Hills, California-based Marti Snider,

owner of A to Z Organizing Services. Snider helps both corporate and individual clients get a handle on their paperwork. "I help them sort through it all," she says, "and I set up
systems for them so they can file things as they come in."
Working side by side with her clients, Snider injects an
objective eye into the organizing process. She helps them
decide what to keep, what to ditch, and how to tell the
difference.

Snider offers a maintenance program as well. ("Just because you set a system up doesn't mean people will use it.")
When organizing isn't enough, Snider can arrange for book-
keepers to come in. She also conducts seminars in time
management.

Snider's clients are mainly small- to mid-size companies
who often don't have the manpower to handle "extra" activities like organization. Though she started out with
mostly individual clients, she prefers the problem-solving
aspect of corporate work.

Snider admits that most clients don't contact her until
they're already in dire straits. "It's hard for people to turn to
someone to handle a job they can do themselves," she says.
"Sometimes, there's an event that precipitates it, like a death
in the family or a divorce." Once they do enlist her services,
though, they're delighted with the results. "When people find
someone who can help them, they're really happy," she says.
"It's like coming home and finding your garage cleaned up
and just the way you want it. It's a real emotional thing."

Snider charges $35 to $45 an hour for her expertise—
rates that are low, she says, for this industry. Many orga-
nizers charge between $75 and $100 an hour. "At this stage
of the game," Snider says, "I don't want to price myself out of
the market."

Snider calls organizing more of a natural talent than a
skill—though it's not a talent that manifests itself in all aspects of her life. "I'm not a fastidious person," she claims. "I
don't think a really fastidious person would have the patience
for this work."

Marketing is the toughest part of starting—and maintaining—an organizing service. Snider recently initiated an ad campaign to keep the flow of new customers coming. Until now, referrals and networking alone have kept her business growing. But other than marketing or advertising costs, this is an inexpensive business to break into. "It's a fun business in the sense that you really don't need anything to get started," Snider says. "I didn't even have business cards for the first six months."

GREETING CARD SENDING SERVICE

Business:

Sending birthday, Christmas, thank-you, and special-occasion cards to the clients/patients of doctors, dentists, shops, and corporations

Basic Equipment and Expenses:

$5,000

Necessities:

Telephone, portfolio of greeting cards, brochures/business stationery, home computer

Experience Required:

None

Inside Tip:

If you're unsure of your market's potential, start out small, like card-sending successes Suzie Clark and Jill Buskirk Johns. Computerizing may be necessary to operate efficiently full-time, but you can try your hand at the business part-time with just a pen and a catalog of cards.

In these days of automated service, remembering a client's birthday with a card can make a big impression. After all, who has time to send personal greetings anymore?

Businesses and busy professionals generally don't have the time. But card-sending services like Albuquerque, New Mexico's CardSenders, certainly do. "We maintain and update our clients' mailing lists for them," explains Suzie Clark, who owns the business with cousin Jill Buskirk Johns. "They choose cards from our portfolio, then we print a handwritten message in each card. The cards get mailed out with a first-class stamp. It's all done so it looks like personal correspondence." Recipients, Clark reports, take the compliments personally. "It's very good for our clients' businesses," she says.

When Clark and Johns started the business in 1985, they were looking for an opportunity that would make money and still leave them time to enjoy life. Johns had heard of a company in California that produced computer-generated cards for local doctors. "We asked them to help us get started," Johns says, "but they didn't think the Albuquerque area warranted that kind of a service."

Johns and Clark weren't so easily discouraged. With a $2,000 investment, they had phone lines installed and brochures printed up. "We envisioned ourselves sitting in front of the television addressing envelopes," Clark says. "That lasted two months, then we realized that the business was there and we needed help." The partners borrowed $10,000 for a computer with custom programming, and the business has been expanding ever since.

CardSenders's ninety clients include insurance agencies, hospitals, real-estate companies, retail shops, general contractors, chiropractors, and dentists. "We started out thinking we'd cater to doctors," Johns laughs, "but we don't have a single physician on our list." Regardless, CardSenders mailed out over 80,000 cards last Christmas.

Johns and Clark say it's possible to start out with a minimal investment of $5,000 for a computer, a portfolio of cards, and basic start-up supplies and licenses. Networking and personal sales calls—not paid advertising—have been the most effective method of spreading the word for these partners. For an additional $5,000, Johns and Clark consult with beginning businesses—helping them set up a system, and giving them access to their exclusive computer software. "It saves them about a year of research and trial and error," Johns says. So far, they've helped seven card-sending services get started across the country.

Other than consulting, the partners have no plans to expand. Each partner works a three-day work week, and both are reluctant to give up that lifestyle. "We would love to expand, but we've become spoiled," Johns says. "I have a two-year-old and a new baby, and my priorities have changed." Money isn't necessarily a motivator for working harder: In 1988 the partners grossed $72,000 working part time—not bad for three days' work.

"One of the reasons we like what we do," Clark adds, "is that it's so flexible. If we decided that we wanted to get aggressive about marketing, the potential is certainly there. We haven't even scratched the Albuquerque market yet."

ETIQUETTE TRAINING

Business:

Coaching professionals on the finer points of dining, demeanor, and public speaking

Basic Equipment and Expenses:

$3,000

Necessities:

Telephone, transportation, marketing brochures/flyers

Experience Required:

Impeccable knowledge of etiquette, good communication skills

Inside Tip:

Your good breeding is probably not enough to make you a professional etiquette coach. Read all the latest books on business and social etiquette—and get some coaching yourself. Your grace, elegance, and style will sell themselves to potential clients.

Phil, 30, has just landed his first executive position. While lunching with an important client, he fumbles over his menu selection, orders an after-dinner cocktail before the meal arrives, and devours the dinner rolls whole from the basket. When the salad comes, he is paralyzed by fork confusion. Phil grew up eating frozen dinners in front of the TV. His understanding of business is impressive, but his knowledge of etiquette is conspicuously lacking. A few social blunders may not cost Phil his job, but they probably will take a toll on the way his associates view him—and the way he views himself.

For years, good manners gave way to a kind of fun informality. Just ten years ago, etiquette was considered stuffy—the dominion of empty rituals and meaningless rules. Now good manners are back, leaving a whole generation to sort out its *p*'s from its *q*'s. They need help, and they're seeking it—both individually and with corporate-backing—from professional etiquette counselors.

"It's no longer enough to be dressed well," argues Washington, D.C., protocol consultant Dorothea Johnson, "and it's no longer acceptable to be a clod." Johnson teaches table manners, social etiquette, and business protocol to high-powered executives, politicians, and diplomats. She claims that good manners can spell the difference between winning and losing in business. "More people are aware of this [today,]" she says, "so they come to me to learn."

Johnson coaches individuals and small groups. Her sessions last four hours each. She also offers a special two-day program called "The Well-Mannered Washington Weekend." What do clients learn? Everything from making their clients feel comfortable to ordering from a menu in French; making introductions and small talk; the correct way to shake hands, give out business cards, send invitations and replies, and leave messages on answering machines; gift giving; the new "female/male" etiquette . . . and more.

According to Johnson, this market is growing fast. But it's more than just a lucrative business. "Sure I make a lot of money," she says. "But the greatest thing is the satisfaction I get from [seeing my clients grow.]"

ON CALL

> Telecommunications consultant Tim Lewis used his smarts instead of his checkbook to create a professional image.

"I could have started out with just a briefcase and someone to call on," says telecommunications consultant Tim Lewis, "but in business, image goes a long way. In order to portray a professional image, I felt I needed an office."

But on Lewis's limited budget, leasing a suite, hiring a secretary, and stocking up on office equipment simply didn't make sense. He needed to devote as much money as possible to developing his new business. Frugality was of the essence—but then, so was establishing credibility.

With a little resourcefulness, Lewis managed both. In 1987, he linked up with the Birmingham Business Assistance Network, an independent, nonprofit business incubator. Through the Network, Lewis secured his own office, and gained access to secretarial help, copiers, postage meters, and a host of equipment and services he could not have afforded otherwise. "It's probably one of the best decisions I made," Lewis says. "It's centrally located and near the interstate, so if I have a job in another city, I'm on the interstate right away."

Connecting with an incubator program wasn't the only smart move Lewis made. He also chose a smart business. When he first started working in the telecommunications field, the best word to describe his clients was "confused." That was shortly after the divestiture of AT&T and, as Lewis puts it, "Consumers had so many options out there that they didn't know what to do." At that time, Lewis was employed by a long-distance telephone company. He was supposed to be selling service, but clients were so baffled by the many equipment and set-up choices they had that they often asked for additional advice. Soon, Lewis realized there was a market for independent and unbiased information—and the idea for T. A. Lewis and Associates was born.

"We show people ways to use their telephone systems more efficiently," explains Lewis. "Sometimes, we design new systems, or help people integrate related services like fax machines or mobile phones into their systems. One of the benefits of using us is that we're able to wade through all the bells and whistles and show people an even apples-to-apples comparison of different equipment. I emphasize training: I make sure that the system is fully operational, and that includes showing people how different features can make their jobs easier."

Lewis started out with two clients—a hospital and a home improvement company. Today, he has twenty to twenty-five active clients at any given time, and business has more than doubled since his first year, 1987. If Lewis is successful, it's no accident. He spent nearly eighteen months researching his market. "You have to spend a lot of time and money on market research to see if you can make money doing what you want to do," he says. Being conscientious is also important. "People always say they want to start a business because they're tired of working for someone else," he laughs. "When you go into business, every client is your boss. You don't work less, you work harder."

16

KIDS, KIDS, KIDS

HOME TUTORING

Business:

Providing supplemental learning opportunities to children and adults

Basic Equipment and Expenses:

$3,000

Necessities:

Teaching materials (you can design your own or buy them through a teaching supply company)

Experience Required:

Varies depending on the type of tutoring you plan to do. For instance, giving piano lessons requires expertise in music. Remedial reading lessons, on the other hand, may call for both teaching and emotional support skills

Inside Tip:

If you're uncertain of your teaching skills, volunteer to help out in a local classroom. You'll develop your teaching abilities and find out firsthand which needs aren't being met in your local schools.

Even the best schools have their limits. Most don't offer courses in specialized subjects: art, music, some foreign languages, certain sports, and so on. Many—especially public schools—can barely handle the basics. One reason is limited funding: District budgets can only pay for so many teachers and so many resources. Another factor is diversity. Public schools must deal with a wide range of special students, from disabled children to immigrants who don't speak English. Perhaps schools can't be all things to all people—but in many cases, they must try to be.

"The schools are good," says educator Irene Breton. "I'm always surprised at the quality of work they're able to do. But they're working with so many people—sometimes they're dealing with two thousand students or more in one school." In these cases, the needs of individual students often are overlooked. "Schools are systems," Breton explains. "Some students have trouble adapting to those systems."

Parents have turned to outside sources for specialized instruction for as long as most of us can remember (recall those weekly piano lessons or your friendly Little League coach). But today, the need for private tutors is more wide-ranging—and more intense.

Breton's Beverly Hills, California-based Breton Educational Centre is living proof. Breton started tutoring from her home. In the beginning, she worked primarily with local children who had special educational needs. She expanded her clientele through referrals from school counselors and psychologists. In two years, the business became so large that she moved into her current facility. Now, she has a "bank" of some twenty tutors—enough to teach "any subject at any level."

Though Breton herself holds a degree in education, she

doesn't require that her tutors have teaching credentials. Enthusiasm and good communication skills take priority. "If a man wants to teach physics and he is an engineer, I may hire him over a teacher," she says, "if he is good with children and is a good communicator." Similarly, you may be able to find a way for yourself in this business without a credential, if you have suitable expertise and a talent for teaching. Training, according to Breton, is critical. Her tutors spend a month learning her special approach to teaching. If you're brand new to teaching, try to get some experience as a classroom aide or part-time tutor before striking out on your own.

Students at the Breton Educational Centre represent a wide range of ages. About 50 percent are elementary school children, 40 percent are teenagers, and the remaining 10 percent are college students and adults. Breton charges $40 an hour for tutoring, and $60 for those requiring special attention. She and her tutors conduct an average of 75 to 100 sessions per week. Though she could easily bring in more business, she is trying to keep the volume manageable. "I like to meet with the parents myself," she explains, "and I meet with my tutors at least once a week."

Despite her success as a businesswoman, Breton seems most proud of her contribution to society as a whole. "The average time a parent spends with a child is seven minutes a day of quality interaction," she says. "One of the benefits of this company is that we put the child with an adult who's there just for them for an hour. Today, that's a gift. Parents can't do it all. We're here to help."

Moreover, Breton has encouraged many failing students to discover the joy of learning. "Almost every day, I receive a letter from a parent who says, 'My child was getting F's in school. After coming to see you, he got D's, then C's,' and so on," she reports. "It's a rare person who can't learn. We tell students they have everything in them to learn; we just have to learn how to work with it.

"It's a simple project," Breton says of her growing company. "It's always a good realization for people to discover the pleasure of learning."

PERSONALIZED CHILDREN'S BOOK PUBLISHING

Business:

Printing and selling personalized children's books

Basic Equipment and Expenses:

$10,000

Necessities:

Home computer with software, stapler

Experience Required:

If starting from scratch, must have writing and illustrating talents. For people without publishing experience, start-up packages are available from several suppliers

Inside Tip:

Not inspired by the children's market? Try marketing personalized books for adults. Using similar techniques, you could create personalized mysteries, adventures, or gothic romances.

Children have always identified with the characters in their favorite books. But thanks to personalized book publishers, getting involved in a book is taking on a whole new meaning to children across the country.

Using computers and special software, it's possible to create children's books that feature a child's name as well as names of friends, family, pets, the home town, and the child's age. You can start from scratch by illustrating your book, having the illustrated pages printed up, then custom printing the text of each book on your computer printer. Or, you can take advantage of personalized publishing programs that already exist on the market.

Karen and John Hefty, founders of Cincinnati, Ohio-based Create-A-Book, began selling personalized children's books in 1979. At that time, personalized children's books already existed, but were sold only through mail order. The Heftys figured they could popularize the concept by selling the books retail. To expand their market, the Heftys started offering distributorships in 1981. Since then, the company has sold over half a million books.

"The books sell for about $12.95," John says. "Dealers can earn as much as $1,000 in a day in high-traffic shopping areas." Shopping malls and swap meets are among the most popular outlets for selling Create-A-Books.

How does it work? Karen, a former reading specialist, writes the books. In all, Create-A-Book offers eleven story-books and one coloring book. The company provides distributors with preprinted pages and covers; distributors print the customized story on the spot. John reports that with a little practice, you can learn to print and assemble a book in about five minutes.

Despite the growth of personalized publishing in recent years—Create-A-Book alone boasts roughly 350 dealerships in the U.S. and another 40 in Canada and Australia—the Heftys maintain that the best is yet to come. "The personalized book business is still in its growth stage," says John. "It is not a novelty that has gone away, it's actually getting bigger."

CHILDREN'S PARTY PLANNING

Business:

Coordinating children's birthday parties, including such services as planning, providing entertainment, catering, and decorating

Basic Equipment and Expenses:

$5,000

Necessities:

Telephone, transportation. Depending on the services you provide, costumes, props, paper goods, party favors, serving equipment, decorations

Experience Required:

Salesmanship, ability to work with and understand children. Must also have a flair for whatever services you plan to provide

Inside Tip:

Be flexible. Parents vary in their willingness to spend on a children's event. Be prepared to do as much—or as little—as they require.

Parents who barely have time to raise their children certainly don't have time to throw birthday parties. Working parents—many of whom are single—often consider their children's parties annual rites of torture. And to make matters worse, today's kids are a savvy bunch. Passing a box of color crayons and dishing out the cake and ice cream simply doesn't thrill.

What can parents do? Send in the clowns. For average fees of $75 to $200, Ann Thomas of Ann's Kids Shows in Baltimore, Maryland, will send in clowns, magicians, story-tellers, puppeteers—anything a kid could want. She will also line up caterers and handle decorations. For more budget-oriented parents, she suggests novel cake designs and do-it-yourself theme parties.

Ann joined her husband's thirty-year-old business, Phil Thomas's Variety Entertainment, sixteen years ago with an eye toward specializing in children's parties. "We had more calls for children's shows than for anything else," she says. Mothers, apparently, are desperate for party help. "They're trying bowling alleys and McDonald's," Ann reports. "In the first place, that's chaos. And in the second place, if they're driving kids around, it's a liability. They can have more fun at home, no matter how small the home is.

"Everything is planned, so there are no slow spots," says Ann. At times, she handles the entertaining herself; other times, she calls on one of twenty part-time entertainers. Apparently, finding talent is no problem. "They find us," she says. "If you list yourself as a party planner, they'll look you up." Screening talent is another matter. Ann and Phil must observe a live performance before they'll consider an enter-tainer. "You can't tell a thing from a tape or audition," Ann contends. "It's the way they work with an audience that counts."

And children are a particular audience. Ann stresses that each child is different, and so is each party. "Sometimes a mother will call me and say she wants a clown for her two-year-old's party. You do not send a costumed character to entertain a two- or three-year-old, unless the party is out-side—then it's a little less threatening," she says. "You have to know these things, and you have to be a good salesperson. You have to be able to convince people that you really know what works, that you really know what you're doing."

Ann plans an average of thirty events per month. These run the gamut from all-day picnics to "sweet sixteen" tea parties. "I don't think there's anyone who puts as much into these parties as we do," Ann reflects. "We sure have a lot of fun."

ALL DRESSED UP

> Margaret Morris and Kathy Hargis never dreamed their trunk of hand-tailored children's costumes could be a viable product—until Neiman-Marcus told them so.

Businesses spend millions marketing new ideas. For many new companies, pitching a new product comprises the largest portion of their start-up expenses. But for Dallas, Texas, entrepreneurs Kathy Hargis and Margaret Morris, start-up marketing didn't cost much. In fact, they made their first major sale before they knew they were in business.

It all started with Hargis's daughter Jennifer Nicole. Hargis and her mother (Morris) wanted to give Jennifer a gift that was neither plastic nor computerized. "We couldn't find a thing," Morris recalls. Finally, Hargis got the idea of buying costumes and putting them in a trunk. Again, they faced defeat. "Everything was so cheaply made," says Morris. "And they were made out of stiff, scratchy fabric. We wanted things that were comfortable. We wanted costumes that would last."

So Hargis and Morris resolved to make costumes themselves. They bought a waitress uniform and scaled it down to a six-year-old's size. They did a princess, a bride, a movie star. "We never did find a trunk," says Morris. But the gift was complete—and a hit. Not only was Jennifer Nicole delighted, but her playmates were also impressed. "Whenever she had a friend over, Kathy got calls asking where they could get costumes like these," says Morris. "One night, she had a slumber party and the next day thirty calls came in. So we said, 'Let's take this idea to Neiman-Marcus and see what they think.' We didn't mean to sell it; we just wanted their opinion."

They got an order instead.

Neiman-Marcus reopened their Christmas catalog to include My Dream Trunk, Hargis and Morris's collection of fully accessorized costumes. Sales exceeded ten times Neiman's original order. Working around the clock—as many as thirty-eight hours straight—the partners managed to deliver 100 percent of the orders by Christmas. "We delivered some of the local orders in person on Christmas Eve," laughs Morris, "but we did it."

Over two years later, the partners are still very much in business. In 1988, they manufactured some 30,000 units for a variety of retailers, including Neiman-Marcus. My Dream Trunks are not cheap: the average price for a trunk with four costumes is over $200. According to Morris, however, the quality is well worth the price. "Every costume is totally accessorized," says Morris. "Our bride has a train of lace, a nosegay with silk flowers, and a forty-two carat "diamond" ring. We have a Victorian Lady, whose dress is made of iridescent English taffeta. This year, we're coming out with King Arthur and Guinevere.

"These costumes are wonderful for children because of their play value," Morris continues. "So many of the toys out there don't encourage role-playing and imagination. Whenever we make a new costume, we run it by our board of directors—the little children who model our clothes. If they don't like them, we won't make them."

17

RETAILING

RETAILING BY KIOSK AND CART

Business:

Hawking your wares at shopping centers and malls from temporary carts and kiosks

Basic Equipment and Expenses:

$7,000

Necessities:

Inventory, cash register if not provided in lease

Experience Required:

None, but be prepared to sell

Inside Tip:

Be frugal in your start-up, but don't skimp on the merchandise. Insider Colleen Higgins urges potential cart and kiosk operators to stock an ample inventory. "I would suggest they start with at least $1,000 to $2,000 in inventory," she says. "You hate to go home with merchandise, but it's hard to sell from a half-full cart."

Don't assume that you can't get into retailing without hundreds of thousands of dollars in capital. It's still possible to start small, and you don't have to locate in a fruit stand off the interstate fifty miles outside the city limits to do it.

Selling your goods from a kiosk or cart is the answer. At shopping centers across the country, entrepreneurs are selling everything from T-shirts to cosmetics, sunglasses to earrings from carts and stands inside the mall itself. For mall developers, these businesses add color and variety to the standard mall format. And for retailers with limited cash, it's an ideal way to make some money, test new products, or launch a lucrative permanent business.

"The start-up costs are so small to get into a cart program," says Colleen Higgins, director of temporary leasing at the Salem Mall in Dayton, Ohio. "It's a great way to get out and test your business. People can rent anywhere from a weekend to a month; we negotiate every month. Some people come in just for special occasions like Mother's Day, Valentine's Day, or Christmas. Others are here year-round."

Mary Golob-O'Sell, owner of the Elegant Express in Davenport, Iowa, uses a kiosk at a local mall on a seasonal basis to boost orders for her gift basket business. Her kiosk is roughly 15 by 20 feet in size, and was constructed for under $1,000, including professional signage. "The mall management's main concern was that the kiosk be tasteful, not tacky," says Golob-O'Sell. "They even came out when I was setting up and offered to provide visual material to create a complete look."

Programs vary from mall to mall. Some malls provide ready-made carts or stands, complete with electrical outlets.

In other cases, you may have to provide some construction work to get your cart operational. Leasing terms also vary. Temporary leases are most common for these types of arrangements, but permanent leases are not unheard of. As cart and kiosk programs catch on at different malls, the variety of options open to you should increase.

What kinds of merchandise can you sell from a cart? Here are just a few of the products that the *Entrepreneur* staff has spotted:

- cappuccino and espresso
- flowers
- sunglasses
- earrings
- stuffed animals and toys
- T-shirts and sweatshirts
- gift baskets
- do-it-yourself bead jewelry
- arts and crafts by local people

The list is virtually endless. The one rule of thumb seems to be selling items that fit the mall's image (nothing cheesy or offensive) and carrying items that regular mall retailers don't. For instance, by offering handmade crafts at your cart, you'll be enhancing the mall's selection without competing with existing shops.

To find out more about opportunities in your area, call the business offices of your local malls. While space and start-up costs may be limited in these ventures, growth potential is not. Floral & Hardy, a flower shop that started out from a Salem Mall cart, now boasts five retail locations.

PACKAGING AND SHIPPING STORE

Business:

Offering the following products and services: moving boxes, gift boxes, gift wrapping, packaging, and shipping

Basic Equipment and Expenses:

$10,000

Necessities:

Retail space, telephone. Inventory includes moving cartons, gift boxes, gift wrap, boxes and plain wrap for mailing, mailing labels, tape, scissors, work area (table, counter)

Experience Required:

None

Inside Tip:

Try out the business on a seasonal basis: Offer Christmas gift-wrapping services from a kiosk at your local shopping mall.

Most stores sell things that go into boxes. These stores sell the boxes themselves. Boxes don't seem like the basis for a successful business, but retailer Leslie Cellucci-Wolf argues otherwise. She and her husband Gary Wolf are co-owners of Cartons Plus, a packaging and shipping store in Torrance, California. "We carry about fifty different-sized cartons for moving," she explains. "We offer packages for shipping, gift wrapping, gift boxes, and packing materials. It doesn't sound like it would keep us busy, but it certainly does."

Cartons Plus addresses a number of different consumer needs. One is the disappearance of cardboard boxes from local supermarkets. At one time, Leslie recalls, you could go to the grocery store for moving boxes. But today, most markets crush these boxes and dispose of them. "Besides," she says. "A lot of people don't want used cartons because they don't know where they've been. Some of them can carry cockroaches." People who are moving themselves have to get their boxes somewhere. And surprisingly, even people who hire moving companies frequent the Wolf's shop. "They have the estimate from the moving company that tells them how many boxes they need, and what size," says Leslie. "Sometimes, they'll buy the boxes from us and do the packing themselves. And sometimes they'll buy the boxes just because we sell them cheaper than the moving company. It's not uncommon for people to spend $200 or $300 on boxes to move a two or three bedroom house."

Gift-wrapping services are also popular at Cartons Plus, especially during the Christmas holidays, when the Wolfs wrap over sixty packages a day. Customers have paid up to $100 for gift wrapping a single package, though a basic wrap starts at $6.25. "The wrapping takes time," Leslie says. "Sometimes it takes an hour and a half to get an elaborate wrap together. We use handmade bows and we make each gift look different."

Packaging and shipping services like Cartons Plus aren't brand new to the world. In fact, they're more popular than you might think. Still, advertising and an accessible location are critical to success. "It takes a long time before you're recognized and known," says Leslie. "We've been in all kinds of Yellow Pages. The advertising will kill you, but if you don't do it, you don't get known."

FLOWER VENDING

Business:

Selling flowers at restaurants, nightclubs, theaters, special events

Basic Equipment and Expenses:

$5,000

Necessities:

Flowers, baskets or other containers, transportation

Experience Required:

Sales/marketing ability

Inside Tip:

Uniforms will give your business a professional image.

Robert Schoolcraft's first day in the flower vending business wasn't especially fun. Armed with $200 worth of flowers in a pickle bucket, he and a single employee set off to the Super Bowl to work the crowd. An agreeable start—only everyone there mistook the pair for cult members. They sold a measly $60 worth of flowers between the two of them. On the way home from the stadium, Schoolcraft's employee announced that flower vending was a dumb idea and would never work.

A first day like that might send most people back to their regular jobs. But Schoolcraft was convinced that his flower-vending business deserved another chance. And he was right. Schoolcraft's Largo, Florida-based Jest Clowns has brought in gross annual sales of over $100,000, and has become the basis for a new game *(Guts: The Game)* and possibly a line of dolls and toys.

Few businesses are simpler than flower vending. To start, you don't need a fancy location, expensive equipment, or tons of inventory. Flower vendors circulate through restaurants, nightclubs, and virtually any other public gathering place, selling single flowers or bouquets from baskets. Overhead is minimal, and experience is not required—though a little chutzpah will help you get your foot in the doors of local businesses. Establishing a "route" is the key to success: most vending operations visit several locations in a single night.

Yet, as Schoolcraft will tell you, flower vending isn't a foolproof business. Image, for one thing, is critical. Many flower vendors wear black cocktail dresses to project an image of elegance. You might say Schoolcraft took the opposite approach. "One of my friends suggested that we dress up like clowns," he says. "I had to try it. I thought that if we were in costume, it would be much easier to gain entrance to restaurants and nightclubs." Ultimately, the idea worked: Schoolcraft's Jest Clowns is now one of the most successful flower vending businesses in the area.

One of the benefits of this business is that you can test the waters yourself without risking a fortune. With a basket and a few dozen flowers, you'll be able to gauge fairly fast how much you like the business—and how well your market likes you. But take a cue from Robert Schoolcraft: Don't quit on your first day out, even if it isn't especially fun.

BURGLAR ALARM SALES AND INSTALLATIONS

Business:

Selling and installing burglar alarms to residential and commercial customers

Basic Equipment and Expenses:

$10,000

Necessities:

Telephone, transportation, tools, supplies

Experience Required:

Licensing requirements vary from state to state, and from city to city. Find out the details from your state and local government

Inside Tip:

Make sure your operations are up to snuff. If you're found negligent, you could have a lawsuit on your hands.

Security is one of the fastest-growing industries in the country. For a relatively low investment, you can cash in on this wave by selling and installing burglar alarms.

To get started, however, you'll need training. Licensing requirements vary locally, so find out first what you'll need to know. According to Patricia Smith, president of the National Burglar and Fire Alarm Association and head of Security, Inc. in Bethesda, Maryland, you may be required to pass a test or to have a master electrician on staff before you can be licensed. Most of the particular knowledge you need is available through classes or work experience.

Smith reports that it's possible to start a burglar alarm company with a relatively low investment, but that professionalism—even on a small scale—is key to survival. "It's not all there in skittles," she warns. "When everyone else is away on vacation, you aren't. You have to be prepared to get a call at three A.M. and respond to it if you expect to stay in business."

On the other hand, it's possible to expand nicely if you're good. "There was a time when we had less than five employees," says Smith. "Now we have ninety-six." Security, Inc. provides installation, service, and monitoring of anything from relatively simple burglar and fire alarms to high-tech card access systems.

Smith credits the company's growth to customer service and financial know-how. Her advice is straightforward: "Don't get overextended financially," she says. "And don't bid low on accounts because you're small. You'll get creamed. Keep your eye on your most important asset: the customer. Give them the best service you can provide. Do an honest job. You'll get referrals and your business will grow."

┃WELL-HEELED SECRET

Consignment retailers Carla Carlson and Daris Birt provide large women with an alternative to expensive boutique clothing.

You might think apparel retailing is out of the question if you're on a limited budget, but Fountain Valley, California, entrepreneur Carla Carlson and Daris Birt don't agree. On a combined investment of $6,000, Carlson and Birt opened the doors of My Secret Place, a used-clothing boutique designed especially for large women.

"We felt there was a demand for this," says Carlson. "These stores go well for other women, but there aren't a lot of large sizes in regular consignment stores."

"And even if there are," Birt adds, "many women don't want to look through a lot of clothing to find something in their size."

Birt and Carlson report that there are a dozen reasons that women buy—and sell—used clothing. Economic incentives on both the buying and selling end are primary. But another common reason is weight fluctuation. "Whether they're gaining or losing," says Birt, "they need transitional clothing." Spending a bundle on new designer, career, and evening wear simply doesn't add up when well-preserved used alternatives are available.

The parners' original $6,000 went toward rent (their shop is in a strip mall), fixtures, advertising, and some new merchandise, mainly lingerie. The partners were able to conserve money by "shopping carefully" for equipment and fixtures, and by getting most of their inventory on consignment.

Though they agree that buying on consignment is a smart way to start, they also note that doing so takes nerve. "We opened the doors and we had no sign and all these empty racks," Carlson says. "It was scary to look at this empty space. It wasn't like we could just call a wholesaler and get the merchandise shipped in. We had to wait for it."

But now—a year later—Carlson and Birt report no problems moving merchandise. The biggest challenge they face is finding cheap, effective ways to get the word out about their business. "Because we're not wealthy women, we have to be careful about where we put our advertising money," Carlson explains. "What we do works well, but we need to figure out what works the best. If we had lots of money, we could try everything. Since we don't, we have to be selective."

"Also, it's very time-consuming," says Birt. "We have many ideas for marketing the business, yet not enough time to implement them." Already, the partners have chipped in over $4,000 in additional funds to keep the business growing at a quick clip. Business at the shop is brisk, the partners say, but they're determined to keep expanding their market.

In that spirit, they're also considering plans to license their concept. "Even now, sixty percent of our customers on a daily basis are new," says Carlson. "There's so much potential in this market, we want to expand the business into new geographical areas."

18

DESIGNING
BUSINESSES

JEWELRY DESIGN AND SALES

Business:

Making and marketing your own jewelry

Basic Equipment and Expenses:

$4,500

Necessities:

Telephone, transportation, merchandise, portable display case, plus any equipment needed to fashion the jewelry itself

Experience Required:

Arts and crafts background helpful, sales skills a definite plus

219

Inside Tip:

Make a point of wearing your jewelry whenever you go out. Follow up compliments with an offer to show your wares.

You don't have to be Paloma Picasso to design your own salable jewelry. Around the country, women are buying up beaded necklaces, bangle bracelets, and ceramic earrings—many of which are made by small-time jewelers. Some of the most interesting and best-selling designs don't even require traditional jewelry-making skills—just a designer's eye and a little inspiration.

Mary Jane Crane of Marblehead, Massachusetts, began making jewelry as a joke. In 1985, she made a pair of clay earrings as a gag gift for a friend. She didn't get laughs; she got requests for more. Today, Crane's business, Earth, Wind, Fire, brings in more orders than she can handle.

Start-up costs were nominal for Crane, who already owned an electric kiln. She had been thinking about selling her ceramics, but couldn't settle on the right product. As it turns out, earrings have advantages that other ceramic wares don't. "I can carry my earrings with me wherever I go," says Crane, "so it's easier to work on them in my free time." In addition to earrings, Crane sells pins, scarf holders, and belt buckles.

Crane's creations are sold in two local shops and a hospital. She and a network of friends also do some direct selling. "I have about ten friends in Boston who bring shoeboxes full of my pieces into their offices and sell them," Crane says. Crane, too, has been known to wield a shoe box. When she first started out, she would bring her pieces to social gatherings, tennis matches, aerobics classes, and the office where she worked. Her eagerness—and reputation—have won her the nickname "the earring lady."

Crane also makes the crafts circuit: "I show my pieces at two big fairs at Christmas and at a spring bazaar every year," she explains. "I create a lot of jewelry for each show, and they usually sell out."

MONOGRAMMING SERVICE

Business:

Monogramming shirts, uniforms, jackets, towels—just about anything that will fit in the machine

Basic Equipment and Expenses:

$10,000

Necessities:

Telephone, monogramming machine

Experience Required:

Marketing ability, no sewing skills required (some operators don't even do the monogramming themselves)

Inside Tip:

Check out local potential for large accounts. Military bases are a good source, since name tapes are standard with every uniform.

According to industry insiders, monogramming is not for handkerchiefs only. In fact, today's monogrammers work on anything from military uniforms to horse blankets. Bowling shirts, restaurant uniforms, corporate perks, and even mattress covers can benefit from the monogrammer's needle. Parkersburg, West Virginia, monogrammer Mary Zinn contracts with local shops for monogramming towels and handkerchiefs but, she says, "Stores will never keep you in business." Corporate and industrial accounts, says Zinn, are the big moneymakers.

Zinn started her monogramming service, Mary's Monograms, in 1984 from a converted home basement. With the help of her husband Vernon (an able handyman and inventor in his own right), she's developed a thriving workshop.

Though the constant demand means long hours for Zinn and her staff, she claims she doesn't mind. "We've worked as many as sixteen hours a day at first," she says. "But the work is so engrossing, you hardly notice the time has passed. You're never bored with it, because every project is different. It's fun to try to duplicate a new logo or design."

Part of what makes monogramming enjoyable—and profitable—is new, computerized equipment. People with little or no sewing experience can learn to monogram quickly and with professional results. Zinn notes that the high-tech equipment does require some brainwork. "You need to be a bit of a mathematician to get everything placed properly," she says. But she mastered the basics in only a day's training and a few weeks' practice.

Zinn does little in the way of promotion. Word of mouth has been most effective in finding clients. She does sponsor a local bowling team (with monogrammed shirts, of course), and she's achieved renown for her beautiful personalized baby blankets. "Whenever I send one to someone out of town, I enclose a business card," says Zinn. "Then they call me for blankets when their friends have babies." Zinn has mailed her blankets as far away as England; orders have come in from across the country.

According to Zinn, the keys to the monogramming business are industry and enthusiasm. "I've never done anything in my life that I've enjoyed more than I do this," she says.

IN STITCHES

Carolyn Curtis thought she was just having a few kids over for informal sewing lessons. Now, she and husband Elbert head a network of over 900 home-based sewing schools.

"We still don't know how the big guys missed this idea," says Carolyn Curtis, president of KIDS CAN SEW in St. George, Utah. "When we looked at the industry, we found that no one was really teaching sewing. They only taught specialty classes to women who already knew how to sew."

But it was kids—namely Carolyn's kids—who expressed an interest in sewing. In 1983, Carolyn's daughters asked her to teach them to sew new clothes for play and school. "The girls asked me to invite a couple of friends to join the class," she says. "Before I knew it, I had parents from the neighborhood calling to see if I'd teach their kids. They even offered to pay me."

Soon, Carolyn was conducting classes every day of the week. She purchased additional sewing machines and took on four students per class at $20 a month working from her home basement. "They're taking sewing off a lot of school programs," she explains, "so this was the only way kids could learn sewing. I also think parents are having fewer children, so they're willing to put more energy and money into activities for them. A lot of parents are working, and like the kids to have something to do after school." That isn't the main thing, however. "The kids really enjoy sewing lessons," Carolyn adds. "If they didn't, they wouldn't keep asking for them."

Carolyn isn't your typical mom teaching classes on the side. She has a degree in fashion merchandising, and has taken courses in both sewing and patternmaking. Ultimately, this training came in handy. Most commercial patterns are difficult for young children to follow, so Carolyn constructed her own. Using simple designs and easy-to-follow instructions, she created patterns that even a six-year-old can use.

Not long after she started teaching, local women started asking how they could start sewing schools of their own. At first, Carolyn helped them out informally. But as her teaching methods grew more sophisticated, she realized that her system was worth money to aspiring instructors. After a little research turned up plenty of evidence to support that suspicion, Carolyn's husband Elbert quit his job as a bank financial manager and joined the firm.

The Curtis's offer packages that help new teachers get their businesses off the ground. The kit contains a teacher training manual, nine beginning KIDS CAN SEW patterns, and advertising slicks, and sells for $60.

"We set up a toll-free number for interested people to call," says Elbert, "and then contacted all the industry publications to get our name out to the women who were looking to make extra money, but didn't want to work outside the home." There were quite a few. Today, there are over 900 KIDS CAN SEW learning centers across the country.

Working with 900 teachers is more than Carolyn bargained for when she invited that first group of students into her home for sewing instructions. But all in all, everything's worked out just fine. "Running a business does run your life," she says. "You have to be in it all the way, or not be in it at all. Luckily, we've been able to involve the whole family, so it's been fun." In fact, the KIDS CAN SEW center at corporate headquarters is run by the Curtis's seventeen-year-old daughter, Teri. Apparently, her mother's lessons really worked.

19

AUTO SERVICES

AUTOMOBILE DETAILING

Business:

Polishing cars with a vengeance: cleaning, waxing, buffing

Basic Equipment and Expenses:

$2,500

Necessities:

Enough space for a work area and ample parking. Tooth-brushes, cotton swabs, rags, high-powered buffers, buckets, soap, wax, and polish

Experience Required:

Patience, attention to detail. No technical training required

Inside Tip:

Try leasing space from an existing automotive business. Car washes are a natural choice, but oil and lube centers or even tire stores are also viable alternatives.

The National Automobile Dealers Association estimates in the early 1990s the average selling price of a new car will climb past $20,000. With prices like these, it's no wonder that more and more car owners are taking care of the cars they have instead of buying new ones.

Yet despite their best intentions, most people are too strapped for time to keep their cars in mint condition. "What it boils down to is that leisure time is becoming a real factor with husbands and wives both working," says R.L. "Bud" Abraham, president of Detail Plus Car Appearance Centers in Portland, Oregon. For many of us, conscientious washing and waxing gives way to a kind of benign neglect—and plenty of guilt.

That's why consumers across the country are having professional detailers go over their cars with high-powered buffers, vacuum cleaners, shampoos, solvents, and even toothbrushes and cotton swabs. Today, approximately 7,000 detailers nationwide gross almost $2.5 million a year.

If detailing sounds like a glorified car wash, that's probably because it is. To get started all you need is ample work space, room to park additional cars, basic car washing and polishing equipment, and a lot of elbow grease. Some companies, like Detail Plus, have sophisticated stainless steel work stations that dispense chemicals and run the equipment. While this equipment may streamline your operations, it will also raise your capital requirements.

Like any business, a successful detailing service depends on steady business. "If you do a good, professional job the first time, you'll not only keep that car's owner coming back, but others as well," says Robert J. Mueller, Jr., president of GEO Polishing Systems in Clearwater, Florida. "People talk about their cars."

In addition to working with individual clients, many detailers look for fleet accounts. Car dealerships, the highway patrol, car rental agencies, city and county agencies, utility companies, school districts, funeral homes, ambulance companies, and any other organization that maintains a fleet of vehicles is a potential client. Wholesale accounts generally don't pay as well as individuals, but they are a steady source of business. Most detailers recommend a combination of both wholesale and retail accounts, especially to start.

For More Information:

Professional Carwashing and Detailing magazine
8 Stanley Circle
Latham, New York 12110
(518) 783-1281

VEHICLE-MOVING SERVICE

Business:

Transporting cars, trucks, and other vehicles from one place to another

Basic Equipment and Expenses:

$10,000

Necessities:

Telephone, insurance, fuel costs

Experience Required:

None

Inside Tip:

If you intend to move cars from state to state, contact the Interstate Commerce Department. You must meet their licensing requirements to operate legally.

"If it has wheels, it probably will need to be moved at some point," says Bill Huber of Auto Driveaway in Columbus, Ohio. Huber's business has transported cars, trucks, cranes, and other sundry vehicles to and from destinations around the country since he bought the firm in 1982. His clients range from large corporations and fleets to individual car owners. Most of his business involves driving vehicles from one place to the next, but Huber will also contract with truckers if the client prefers.

Clients call Huber for any number of reasons. Many move across the country by plane (and moving van) and need their cars delivered. In other cases, rental-car agencies need cars moved from one agency to another. Company cars get shuttled between offices. Car dealerships exchange cars. Military vehicles need transporting. Like Huber says, "All kinds of people need to get cars from point A to point B."

Huber has twelve regular drivers and a long list of independent contractors. Independents don't get paid per se: Their compensation is the use of the car. "We're providing them with transportation and a tank of gas," says Huber. For cross-country jaunts, Auto Driveaway suggests routes and stops. "We plan their whole trips for them," he says. He finds most of his drivers through referrals and occasional newspaper ads. Only rarely has Huber had a problem driver. "We have a good screening process," he explains, "and they have to leave a security deposit. Once in a great while we might have a problem, but that's what insurance is for."

In a year, Huber moves about 700 vehicles. He characterizes his operation as "mid-sized" for the business. His Columbus, Ohio location is part of a nationwide network based in Chicago—an organization that Huber says has helped him learn the business and attract a national clientele. In addition to the cars he's moved, Huber has made arrangements for 200 more annually through some of the eighty-five other Auto Driveaways in the network. "For me to move cars from Seattle to Denver, I need that network," Huber says. Starting an independent moving service is possible, he says, if you're willing to stick to locally generated business.

Otherwise, it's important simply to be a good businessperson. "If you're going to offer a service, you better offer a good service," Huber advises. "You have to know how to sell and how to treat people right."

WINDSHIELD REPAIR SERVICE

Business:

Repair cracked and pitted auto windshields

Basic Equipment and Expenses:

$2,500

Necessities:

Telephone, transportation, windshield repair equipment and materials

Experience Required:

None. Most equipment comes with instructions and/or training

Inside Tip:

Low initial investment and flexible hours make this an appealing business for students, retirees, and part-timers.

Repairing a windshield can cost you $25 to $40. The average cost of replacement is over $200. Therein lies the appeal of the windshield repair business: It's as simple as saving money.

If you haven't heard of windshield repair, you aren't alone. Though commercial dealerships and fleets have been repairing windshields for years, consumers are just now discovering this service.

How do you repair a windshield? The process involves three basic steps: vacuuming the air from the damaged area, injecting an optically clear resin into the gap, and allowing the resin to cure. The entire process takes just ten to fifteen minutes. And by most accounts, you needn't be a mechanical genius to become a crack technician. Equipment and supply packages are available from a number of manufacturers, and most include instruction on doing the repairs.

Dave Gittins of Glass Mechanix in southwest Florida got into the business through a Sunrise, Florida, company called Glass Mechanix. He launched the business while still working full-time. Within three months, he had enough business to quit his job and devote all his energies to marketing and repairs.

In Gittins's case, those energies were considerable. "Before I even started, I felt out the need for a service like this in my area," he says. "Then when I started the business, I began creating a need for it. People don't know about windshield repair, so I did work for free to show them how valuable it was."

Most of Gittins's business comes from commercial accounts: car dealerships and fleets. Companies that maintain a lot of vehicles (car rental agencies, delivery services, limousine companies, even the U.S. Postal Service) represent a lucrative market for the windshield repairperson. Not only are they anxious to save money, but they also offer potential for repeat business.

In order to build these contacts, you must be an enthusiastic salesperson and a conscientious businessperson. "There are some people out there who are not doing a good job," Gittins says, "and they're damaging the industry." Ultimately, they're also damaging their own businesses—without steady clients, marketing can be an uphill battle.

With steady clients, a windshield repairperson can expect good returns on a fairly low investment. According to Gittins, a new operator in a small town can expect to gross $29,000 to $32,000 in the first year. With aggressive marketing and continuous work, $60,000 a year is not unthinkable.

But before you jump into the windshield repair business, Gittins suggests shopping around. "I recommend that people get some hands-on experience," he says. Look for an established service (perhaps in another part of the country) that you can observe for a week or so. "It's hard to really understand this business until you see it," says Gittins. "Find out as much as you can before you start."

USED-CAR INSPECTIONS

Business:

Inspecting used cars for prospective buyers

Basic Equipment and Expenses:

$5,000

Necessities:

Telephone, transportation, testing equipment for cars

Experience Required:

Must have thorough knowledge of car mechanics

Inside Tip:

Test your market: take out an ad in the shopping news, where many people shop for used cars.

As a used car buyer, the consumer has two people to consult: the used car salesman and the friendly mechanic. It's a lot like being stuck between a rock and a hard place. What the used-car buyer needs is an educated, unbiased evaluation. But until now, finding that kind of information hasn't been easy.

At Car Checkers of America in Edison, New Jersey, clients get a complete rundown of a car's strengths and weaknesses. Wendy Mandell and Lee Geller, former used-car wholesalers, offer inspections and appraisals for people buying used vehicles. For $49.95, Geller or one of his technicians will inspect more than 275 items on a used car before the purchase is made, and will give the customer a written evaluation and recommendation. "If the car meets our qualifications, we can also [guarantee] it for up to two years or 40,000 miles through an insurance company," Geller says.

The partners thought up the idea for an objective evaluation service when Geller sold his car to a neighbor. "I knew the car needed new brakes," he says, "so I had our mechanic put them in and encouraged my friend to have her mechanic inspect the car. He said the car needed new brakes, and wanted to charge her $175 to put them in."

First-year sales at Car Checkers topped $100,000. The partners used the money to move from a home-based office to commercial space. They're so optimistic about the market for their services that they're currently franchising their business. Though total start-up costs for a Car Checkers franchise can run as high as $19,000, it is possible to open your own Car Checkers from home for about $10,000, including the cost of national advertising and business insurance.

TAKING THE HIGH ROAD

Dan Hill could cut corners and take home an extra $100,000 a year. But this automotive entrepreneur believes that offering the best equipment and treating his employees right will reap bigger rewards in the long run.

Lawndale, California, entrepreneur Dan Hill, Sr. knows what it's like to start a business with slim funds. In 1985, he went into the business of installing car alarms. "For $125, we bought a two-line telephone and started out of the garage," he says. Hill made the sales calls to car dealerships: His son Dan, Jr. and a friend did the installations. From these humble beginnings, Venco Distributing, Inc. was born.

From the start, Hill was hellbent on integrity. "There are a lot of carpetbaggers in this business," he says. "I don't want to do business that way. Our company is not highly profitable, but by design. Not having great financial resources, we need to put every dollar we can back into the business."

And that he has. Since his early garage days, Hill has bought out a retail location, acquired a sunroof company, and begun to dabble in cellular car phones and even race cars. Sales in the car alarm division have grown from $200,000 his first year to about $1.8 million in 1988. Similarly, the sunroof business has blossomed from $60,000 in 1985 to $500,000 in 1988—and 1989 sales should approach $1 million.

Hill's secret: careful management and a capable, motivated staff. He's a fan of efficiency—even at a price. "We put a lot of money into computers and software development," he says, "so we can keep track of our business. Now, I can follow trends in a dealer's business [through the computer]. I've been able to predict a little ahead of time when business was going to take a downturn. When that happens, we can cut our expenses to prepare."

But cost-cutting does not happen at the expense of employees. "When times are slow, we don't lay off our employees like just about everyone else does," he says. "If they have to sit around and play cards because there's no work, they'll get paid for it. We figure if they're good enough to work here, we want them to stay around for when we are busy." In an industry where paid benefits are rare, Hill provides health and dental insurance, worker's compensation, and payroll taxes. His salaries—and hence his expenses—are high, but he insists the investment is worthwhile. "We've dealt with tens of thousands of people, and I've been able to count on my employees to deal with every one of them well," he explains. "I could cut out the benefits and take home another $100,000 or $200,000 right there. But without this kind of staff, it would be hard to build the kind of business I want."

The kind of business Hill wants is diversified. Bit by bit, he's added new products and services to the agenda. Installing car alarms is still a major focus, but alarms alone aren't the ultimate goal. "I want people to think of Venco as the place to call if they need something for their car," Hill says. "I want them to say, 'Call Venco, they can probably help you.'"

New ideas come naturally to Hill, who likes to contemplate business over a good game of pinball. "I have two pinball machines in the office," he says. "Those have been the greatest inspiration to me. I don't go to lunch: I play pinball." According to Hill, innovation is a logical extension of doing business. "It's like dominoes," he says. "As more things happen, more ideas build up. Things fall into your lap just because you're there."

Of course, that doesn't mean it's easy. Hill assesses his competition as "decades behind" his company. Installing high-grade equipment and maintaining a quality staff costs money. And conscientiousness tends to feed on itself. "Our image bears a certain burden," says Hill. "People expect us to be the best. When our competitors make mistakes, people deal with it. When we make mistakes, people are all over us." Still, he would never exchange his reputation for a fast buck. Hill may not finish last, but he is a good guy.

20

ODDS AND ENDS

TRANSLATION SERVICE

Business:

Translating documents into and out of foreign languages

Basic Equipment and Expenses:

$5,000

Necessities

Telephone, transportation, office space; home computer with word processing helpful

Experience Required:

Must be fluent in English and one other language. To be a successful translator, you need a high level of proficiency in both languages, and preferably some experience in actual translation

Inside Tip:

All languages are not created with equal demand. Find out if the demand for the language you know will support a full-time business in your area.

Want to improve international relations? Become a professional translator and help businesses, government agencies, and private individuals understand their foreign counterparts more clearly.

Shuckran Kamal, a Herndon, Virginia, translator reports that a wide range of jobs are available to skilled translators. Kamal herself translates legal and personal documents, promotional materials, instruction manuals, and even food labels from English to Arabic, and vice versa in the metropolitan Washington, D.C., area. About the only type of translation she doesn't do is technical documents that require special expertise.

Kamal stresses that good translation is not as simple as converting words from one language into another. "The sentence structure varies from language to language," she says. "There is a lot of figurative language. There can be innuendos, satire. You have to be able to ferret out the meaning." To be able to do that, you must have a strong command of both languages, as well as a good dose of writing ability. While Kamal believes "translation is a skill that you acquire by doing," she also recommends taking classes in translation before getting into the business to get some preliminary guidance. Beyond that, she urges aspiring translators to read widely in their second language to gain an intuitive feeling for it.

Established translators earn anywhere from $25 to $65 an hour or more for editing and evaluation services. For actual translation, rates range from $5 per 100 words to as much as $15 or $20 per 100 words, depending on the language, the type of document, and the translator's experience. Finding work isn't difficult, according to Kamal, but maintaining a steady work flow can be tricky at first. Word of mouth and referrals from professional contacts are most productive in attracting new accounts.

Kamal is a particular proponent of professional associations. As a member of the American Translator's Association, she's found a network of colleagues that are a valuable source of information and support. "For people like myself who freelance, it's difficult to find colleagues to discuss business with," Kamal says. "That's why a professional association is so useful. We live and work in isolation. Sometimes the annual meeting is the only time we can talk about our businesses."

PRIVATE INVESTIGATING

Business:

Locating missing persons, finding missing heirs, investigating insurance fraud cases, tracking down people who are delinquent on loans, running background checks on prospective employees, screening potential tenants, recovering people who have skipped bail—in short, all varieties of tracking down information

Basic Equipment and Expenses:

$6,500

Necessities:

Telephone, transportation

Experience Required:

None. Persistence and smarts are essential in this business. In some states, you will need a license to operate. Check with your state government for details

Inside Tip:

As a P. I. your hours will be flexible but long. At times, you may have to work weekends or into the wee hours of the morning. Don't pursue this business if you're a dedicated nine-to-fiver.

Here's your chance to put those keen investigative instincts to work. According to the National Association of Investigative Specialists (NAIS), the number of investigators in the United States is increasing by 10 to 15 percent annually. And not only is the field growing, but it's also lucrative. The NAIS estimates that today's average agency grosses between $75,000 and $100,000 with net profits of 75 percent.

If this sounds like your kind of business, maybe it is. But don't expect a life of glamour, intrigue, excitement, and suspense. As a private investigator, you probably won't find yourself in the midst of high-speed chases and life-threatening shootouts. In fact, most of your work will take place in offices. So unless turning on your computer or combing files at the county courthouse makes your pulse rush, do not go into this business for the sheer thrill of it.

Do, however, consider this business if you're persistent, thorough, smart, and resourceful—these are the skills you'll need on this job. Investigative experience is not required, just a knack for getting the facts.

Fay Faron, owner of Rat Dog Dick in San Francisco, credits a leaky houseboat with the start of her agency. "Six weeks after I bought the houseboat, it sank," she explains. Faron confronted the former owner, but he refused to give her compensation. To prove that the boat was already damaged when she bought it, Faron had to locate the former tenant. "I found him in just two days, even though he had changed his name and moved to Texas," Faron says. "My attorney was so impressed that he gave me the names of three people who owed him money on judgments and said, 'If you find them, I'll give you half the money.'" Faron found them, and set off on a new career path.

Locating missing persons for loved ones (or creditors) is a common specialty among private investigating firms. Another is running background checks on prospective employees. Some especially brave P.I.s opt for bounty hunting—recovering individuals who have skipped bail. For newcomers, it's possible to get into the P.I. business even without clients. P.I.s can check courthouse records to look at files of missing heirs and unclaimed property which, according to the federal government, amounts to more than $25 billion in unclaimed assets. The investigator who finds the missing heir or property owner then charges them a finder's fee of up to 50 percent of the property's value.

"If I were going into business today, I would probably go into background checks, asset searches, things like that," says Pat Rutherford, director of Worldwide Tracers, a three-office P. I. firm based in San Clemente, California. "Those are the easy [investigations] to start with, and they're so necessary to people in business."

Overhead is minimal in the P. I. business. Working from home is not only possible, but given the irregular hours that most private investigators work, it's often desirable. Though splurging on a number of high-tech devices might be tempting at first, bare-bones equipment shouldn't empty your bank account. In some states, private investigators must be licensed. To avoid any legal hassles down the road, check with your state government to see what the requirements are, if any.

Though the private investigating field is growing these days, it's certainly not impacted. Rutherford calls the opportunities in this field, "wide open." If you think you have the right skills for sleuthing, investigate the market in your area. You may find yourself on the trail of a major success.

For More Information:

National Association of Investigative Specialists
P.O. Box 33244-EN
Austin, Texas 78764
(512) 832-0355

A MAN AND HIS BIKES

When cyclist Greg Miller found out he couldn't go to the Moscow Olympics, he had "no money and nothing to do." He started a bicycle repair shop with a meager investment and found big financial and personal returns.

The good news was, he made the Olympic team. But that good news didn't amount to much when the U.S. decided to boycott the Moscow Olympics and cyclist Greg Miller lost his chance to compete. After working in a bike shop for six years and training like crazy for races, Miller had few skills beyond his genuine love of bicycles—so he used that to start a business.

"I convinced my dad to help me turn my apartment into a bike shop," he says. Armed with just his tools, a newspaper ad, and a hand-held floor pump, he took in repairs from his Seal Beach, California, living room and ran his personal life from the back of the shop. "People would bring their bikes in and smell dinner cooking," he laughs. "Finally, the business got so big, it kicked me out."

Miller works on all types of bikes, from rusty beach cruisers to top-of-the-line racing models. "Basically, a bike is a bike," he says. "It's not hard to learn bicycle repair, but there is a difference between doing a perfect job and doing a basic job. I like to do exceptional work all the time." Miller's reputation for quality helps him win high-end business— that and his racing expertise, of course.

Because of this racing experience, he was also able to land a job doing bicycle repair for the 7-Eleven team in the Tour de France. "I go to France for a month every year to do that," he says. Working at the race (not to mention in France) gives Miller a real charge. And it hasn't hurt his credibility, either. He is one of only two American repair people who have worked at the Tour de France. "It's been unbelievable for the business," he reports. "People know I'm not just a kid fixing bikes."

As the business grows, Miller is cautious about expanding. So far, it's just him and one assistant holding down the fort. In addition to repairs, Miller also sells bikes and equipment retail. "I couldn't have afforded that in the beginning," he says. "You have to buy all your inventory and I sell $3,000 bikes. My first year in business, I think I made $3,000." These days, however, he's doing considerably better. In 1988, he made a $100,000 profit.

"People don't think you can make money in the bike business," Miller says. "That hasn't been true for me." Starting small may have helped. "Other people have high overhead and lots of employees," he explains. "I've kept my business small, so I can go with seasonal changes in the industry— they don't wipe me out. I've thought about expanding, but then I wouldn't be able to do what I want," like taking his annual trip to France or participating in the Race Across America in a covered bike. As it is, he complains of not getting his hands greasy on repairs as much as he'd like.

Miller doesn't bill himself as a business prodigy. In fact, he admits to getting plenty of advice from his CPA father. "You should see him at tax time," Miller confides. "I'm so bad about taxes that he can't believe it."

But he does have a real way with bikes. It's the kind of enthusiasm that can't be fabricated, and customers really seem to appreciate it. "I talk directly with them about their bikes," he says. "I show them how to change a tire if they want. It's a real hands-on feeling they get at the shop. I'm lucky to be in the bike business because I really love it. I'm here seven days a week and it isn't even like work. I really enjoy what I'm doing. I really love bikes."

165 Guides to Help You Start Your Own Business

ANIMAL-ORIENTED BUSINESSES

Business Guide No. ....Reg. Price/Sub. Disc.
1033. Pet Hotel & Grooming Service $69.50/59.50
1007. Pet Shop $69.50/59.50

APPAREL BUSINESSES

Business Guide No. ....Reg. Price/Sub. Disc.
1161. Children's Clothing Store $69.50/59.50
1272. Large-Size Women's Apparel Store $29.50
1152. Lingerie Shop $69.50/59.50
1290. "Sweats"-Only Retailing $69.50/59.50
1043. T-Shirt Shop $69.50/59.50
1229. Used/Consigned Clothing.............$69.50/59.50
1333. Women's Accessories Store $69.50/59.50

1107. Women's Apparel Shop $69.50/59.50

AUTOMOTIVE BUSINESSES

Business Guide No. ....Reg. Price/Sub. Disc.
1076. Car Wash $69.50/59.50
1268. Cellular Phone Service $69.50/59.50
1146. Detailing, Automobile ....$69.50/59.50 †
1224. Limousine Service $69.50/59.50
1054. Oil-Change, 10-Minute $69.50/59.50
1197. Parts Store, Auto $69.50/59.50
1018. Sales, Consignment $29.50
1108. Used-Car Rental Agency $69.50/59.50
2330. Used Car Sales ....$69.50/59.50 ‡
2329. Vehicle Leasing ....$69.50/59.50 ‡

What's inside an Entrepreneur How-to Business Guide:

Imagine having a group of business owners unselfishly confide the details of their success in the kind of business you want to start. They reveal profits and operating costs. They share their solutions to typical problems. They give you their own secrets for making the business "hum".

That's what it's like inside an Entrepreneur Business Guide. You get inside information compiled, analyzed and categorized by our staff and put in a form that's easy to read and understand. It gives you the equivalent knowledge of many years of experience in your new business even though you're just starting out.

Each Guide is approx. 200 pages in length, and comes full tabbed for easy reference in its own handsome, vinyl-covered loose leaf binder.

YOU LEARN–

■ The profit potential for this business ■ The specific start-up costs ■ The size and scope of the market ■ How many hours a week it will take ■ How to easily manage this type of business ■ Site selection and lease negotiation ■ What kind of equipment you may need ■ Anticipated sales volume ■ Sample floor layout of your operation ■ How and where to buy supplies ■ How to set prices ■ How to set up an accounting system ■ Licenses and permits you may need and where to get them ■ How to hire and set up payroll when you're ready ■ How to advertise and promote your type of business.

Each guide comes with an unconditional 90-day money back guarantee (from date of purchase, less shipping and handling).

**CALL TOLL FREE 1-(800) 421-2300
in California 1-(800) 352-7449**

COMPUTER-ORIENTED BUSINESSES

Business Guide No. ....Reg. Price/Sub. Disc.

2335. Bookkeeping Service $69.50/59.50
1221. Consulting &
Temporary-Help Service, ...$69.50/59.50
1288. Desktop Publishing $69.50/59.50
2333. Diet & Meal Planning...................$69.50/59.50
1084. Hardware Store, Computer $69.50/59.50
1265. Home Computer,
Making Money With a $69.50/59.50
1237. Information Broker $69.50/59.50
1256. Repair Service, Computer $69.50/59.50
1253. Software Locator Service $69.50/59.50
1261. Software Store $69.50/59.50
2332. Tax Preparation Service................$69.50/59.50

CRAFT & MANUFACTURING BUSINESSES

Business Guide No. ....Reg. Price/Sub. Disc.

1304. Craft Businesses $64.50/54.50
1262. PVC Furniture Mfg $64.50/54.50

EMPLOYMENT SERVICES

Business Guide No. ....Reg. Price/Sub. Disc.

1051. Employment Agency $69.50/59.50
1228. Executive Recruiting Service $69.50/59.50
1260. Resume Writing &
Career Counseling $69.50/59.50
1189. Temporary-Help Service $69.50/59.50

FAST-FOOD BUSINESSES

Business Guide No. ....,. ...Reg. Price/Sub. Disc.

1270. Chicken, Flame-Broiled $29.50
1083. Cookie Shop $69.50/59.50
1126. Donut Shop $69.50/59.50
1073. Hamburger/Hot Dog Stand $69.50/59.50
1187. Ice Cream Store $69.50/59.50
**1056. Mobile Restaurant/
Sandwich Truck $29.50**
1006. Pizzeria $69.50/59.50
1279. Restaurant Start-Up $69.50/59.50
1079. Yogurt (Frozen) Shop $69.50/59.50

FOOD & SPIRITS, RETAIL

Business Guide No. ....Reg. Price/Sub. Disc.

1158. Bakery $69.50/59.50
1202. Coffee & Tea Store $69.50/59.50

1173. Convenience Food Store $69.50/59.50
1296. Health-Food/Vitamin Store $69.50/59.50
1024. Liquor Store $69.50/59.50
1295. Muffin Shop $29.50

HOMEBASED BUSINESSES

Business Guide No. ....Reg. Price/Sub. Disc.

1278. Bed & Breakfast Inn $69.50/59.50
1288. Desktop Publishing $69.50/59.50
1258. Freelance Writing $69.50/59.50
1306. Gift Basket Service ....$69.50/$59.50
1265. Home Computer,
Making Money With $69.50/59.50
1092. Import & Export $69.50/59.50
1015. Mail-Order Business $69.50/59.50
1308. Silk Plants ....$67.50/59.50 †

HOME FURNISHINGS

Business Guide No. ....Reg. Price/Sub. Disc.

1212. Used/Consignment Furniture Store $69.50/59.50

PERSONAL SERVICES

Business Guide No. ....Reg. Price/Sub. Disc.

1194. Dating Service $69.50/59.50
1170. Hair Salon, Family $69.50/59.50
1264. Image Consulting $69.50/59.50
1274. Nail Salon $69.50/59.50
1239. Tutoring Service $29.50
1330. Wedding Planning Service $69.50/59.50

PHOTO-RELATED BUSINESSES

Business Guide No. ....Reg. Price/Sub. Disc.

1209. One-Hour Photo Processing Lab $69.50/59.50
1204. Videotaping Service $69.50/59.50

PUBLISHING BUSINESSES

Business Guide No. ....Reg. Price/Sub. Disc.

1067. Newsletter Publishing $69.50/59.50

RECREATION & ENTERTAINMENT BUSINESSES

Business Guide No. ....Reg. Price/Sub. Disc.

1242. Balloon Delivery Service $69.50/59.50
1186. Bar/Tavern $69.50/59.50
1269. Bowling Center $69.50/59.50
1308. Compact Disc-Only Store $69.50/59.50
1132. Hobby Shop $69.50/59.50

**CALL TOLL FREE 1-(800) 421-2300
in California 1-(800) 352-7449**

1342. Mobile DJ $69.50/59.50
1124. No-Alcohol Bar $69.50/59.50
1100. Pinball & Electronic Game Arcade $69.50/59.50
1226. TV & Movie Production $69.50/59.50
1192. Videocassette Rental Store $69.50/59.50

RESTAURANTS, SIT-DOWN

Business Guide No. ....Reg. Price/Sub. Disc.
1289. Diner...$69.50/59.50
1279. Restaurant Start-Up $69.50/59.50
1156. Sandwich Shop/Deli $69.50/59.50

RETAIL BUSINESSES, MISC.

Business Guide No. ....Reg. Price/Sub. Disc.
1318. Baby Store $69.50/59.50
1277. Beauty Supply Store $69.50/59.50
1293. Bookstore, Children's ....,......$69.50/59.50
1331. Character Merchandise Store $29.50
1135. Cosmetics Shop $69.50/59 50
3361 Buying Products
      From Other Countries $59.50/49.50
1143. Flower Shop ....,,,.......$69.50/59.50
1144. Framing Shop, Do-It-Yourself $69.50/59.50
1306. Gift Basket Service ....$69.50/59.50 †
1218. Gift, Specialty Store $69.50/59.50
1323. Kiosks & Cart
      Business Opportunities... ....$69.50/59.50
1222. Multilevel Marketing Sales,
      How to Develop $69.50/59.50
1316. Off-Price Retailing $29.50
1283. Party Goods/Gift Store $69.50/59.50
1325. Print/Poster Store $69.50/59.50
1214. Religious-Gift/Book Store $69.50/59.50
1340. Sock Shops...............................$69.50/59.50
1337. Silk Plants Shop ....$69.50/59.50 †
1322. Sports Memorabilia Store $69.50/59.50
1117. Used-Book Store $69.50/59.50
1182. Wedding Shop $69.50/59.50

SELF-IMPROVEMENT BUSINESSES

Business Guide No. ....Reg. Price/Sub. Disc.
1172. Physical-Fitness Center $69.50/59.50
1046. Self-Improvement/Insight-
      Awareness Seminars $69.50/59.50

SERVICES TO BUSINESS

Business Guide No. ....Reg. Price/Sub. Disc.
1223. Advertising Agency $69.50/59.50
1292. Advertising, Specialty $69.50/59.50
1236. Apartment Preparation Service $69.50/59.50
1317. Business Brokerage $69.50/59.50
1307. Business Development Center........$69.50/59.50
1207. Collection Agency $69.50/59.50
2328. Construction Cleanup ....$69.50/59.50 ‡
1329. Construction Interior Cleaning,
      New $69.50/59.50
1151. Consulting Business $69.50/59.50
1232. Coupon Mailer Service $69.50/59.50
1328. Freight Brokerage $69.50/59.50
1237. Information Broker $69.50/59.50
1336. Instant Sign Store $69.50/59.50
1034. Janitorial Service $69.50/59.50
1098. LiquidatorSelling
      Distressed Merchandise $69.50/59.50
1332. Mobile Bookkeeping Service ....,,$69.50/59.50
1962. Money Broker $84.50/74.50
1031. Parking Lot Striping &
      Maintenance Srvc $69.50/59.50
1280. Pest Control $69.50/59.50
1324. Public Relations Agency $69.50/59.50
1339. Referral Services...........................$69.50/59.50
1136. Secretarial/
      Word-Processing Service $69.50/59.50
1150. Surface Cleaning, Mobile $69.50/59.50
1148. Telephone-Answering Service $69.50/59.50
1157. Trucking, Cross-Country $69.50/59.50
1012. Window-Washing Service $69.50/59.50

SERVICES TO THE HOME

Business Guide No. ....Reg. Price/Sub. Disc.
1053. Carpet-Cleaning Service $69.50/59.50
1215. Catering Service $69.50/59.50
1291. Closet Customizing $69.50/59.50
1334. Home Inspection Service $69.50/59.50
1275. House Sitting/In-Home Care $29.50
1314. Interior Designer..........................$69.50/59.50
1105. Kitchen Remodeling $69.50/59.50
1198. Lawn-Care Service $69.50/59.50
1343. Mini-Blind Cleaning $69.50/59.50
1160. Maid Service $69.50/59.50
1249. Painting, House $69.50/59.50

1285.	Pool Cleaning & Repair $69.50/59.50
1012.	Window-Washing Service $69.50/59.50

SERVICE BUSINESSES, MISC.

Business Guide No. ....Reg. Price/Sub. Disc.

1309.	Check Cashing Service $69.50/59.50
1058.	Child-Care Service $69.50/59.50
1037.	Dry-Cleaning Shop $69.50/59.50
1313.	Event Planning Service $69.50/59.50
1306.	Gift Basket Service $69.50/59.50
1298.	Instant Print/Copy Shop $69.50/59.50
1326.	**Instant Shoe Repair Shop $29.50**
1162.	Laundromat $69.50/59.50
1042.	Mini-Storage Facility $69.50/59.50
1287.	Packaging & Shipping Service $69.50/59.50
1310.	Personal Shopping Service $69.50/59.50
1341.	Pet Sitting $69.50/59.50
1320.	Private Investigator $69.50/59.50
1147.	Private Mailbox Service $69.50/59.50
1335.	Senior Day Care $69.50/59.50
1150.	Surface Cleaning, Mobile $69.50/59.50
1154.	Travel Agency $69.50/59.50
1077.	~~Vinyl-Repair Service~~ **$29.50**

SPORTS BUSINESSES

Business Guide No. ....Reg. Price/Sub. Disc.

1022.	**Bicycle/Moped Shop $29.50**
1286.	Sporting-Goods Store $69.50/59.50
1322.	Sports Memorabilia Store $69.50/59.50

STREET-VENDING BUSINESSES

Business Guide No. ....Reg. Price/Sub. Disc.

3360	Sourcebook of Products for Flea Markets.............................$59.50/49.50
1127.	Shrimp Peddling $64.50/54.50
1299.	Vending Businesses $69.50/59.50

MISCELLANEOUS BUSINESSES

Business Guide No. ....Reg. Price/Sub. Disc.

1091.	Burglar Alarm Sales/ Installation ...$69.50/59.50
2327.	Buying Foreclosures ....$69.50/59.50 ‡
1227.	Government Contracts, How to Obtain $69.50/59.50
1282	Herb Farming $69.50/59.50
1222.	Multilevel Marketing Sales, How to Develop $69.50/59.50
1153.	Real Estate Company, Flat-Fee $69.50/59.50
1284.	Real Estate, Complete Investment Guide $69.50/59.50
1071.	Seminar Promoting $69.50/59.50

IMPROVING YOUR BUSINESS ABILITY

Business Guide No. ....Reg. Price/Sub. Disc.

3402.	Business Plan, Developing A $59.50/49.50
7205.	Calif. Business Start-Up $64.50/54.50
3370	Complete Government Resource Guide Complete Set $99.50/89.50
3371	Western Region $49.50/39.50
3372	Midwestern Region....................$49.50/39.50
3373	Southern Region $49.50/39.50
3374	Eastern Region $49.50/39.50
1321.	Credit Consulting $69.50/59.50
7000.	Incorporation Kits for Any State (Specify State) $59.50/49.50
1327.	Lessons From America's Successful Entrepreneurs $54.50/44.50
1312.	Personal Financial Planner $84.50/74.50
1111	Promotional Gimmicks $69.50/59.50
1999.	Complete Library of All Business Guides.................$5,450/$4,450
1315.	SBA Loan Guide $74.50/64.50
1319.	Standard Business Forms for the Entrepreneur $59.50/49.50

‡ Audio Cassettes Plus Reference Book

† Supplemental Video available

Satisfaction Guaranteed

You have nothing to lose. If you follow the instructions and they do not work for you, return the business guide within 90 days with a simple note, telling us where we went wrong. Yes, return the business guide within 90 days and we'll return the purchase price, less shipping and handling.

Place your order by mail or phone.

To order by phone:
Call TOLL FREE: 1(800)421-2300
CA residents call: 1(800)352-7449

For rush shipments:
Please call our toll free number:
6a.m.-8:30p.m. Monday-Friday
7a.m.-3p.m. Saturday Pacific Coast time.

For customer service or billing inquiries call:
1(800)345-8614
In CA call: (714)261-2325 • 8a.m.-5p.m. • Monday-Friday

To Order by phone: ☎

In order to save you time when ordering, please have the following information ready:

1. Completed order form.
2. Credit card number and expiration date.
3. Customer code number: **9N184**
4. Please note: We do not take C.O.D. orders.

To Order by Mail: ✉

1. Be sure to fill out the order form completely.
2. Please check all your entries for legibility.
3. Please include a home <u>and</u> work phone number in case we have a question about your order.
4. Be sure to include your complete street address for parcel deliveries. U.P.S. will not deliver to P.O. boxes.

**CALL TOLL FREE 1-(800)421-2300
in California 1-(800)352-7449**

ORDER FORM

Entrepreneur Business Guides

Save up to 20% on Entrepreneur Guides when you subscribe to *Entrepreneur Magazine*

Guide #	Guide Title	Price

California Residents add 6.25% sales tax	
Add $6.75 for shipping and handling	
Add $2.00 shipping and handling for each additional business guide	
Entrepreneur subscription fee	
Canadian orders add $15.50 shipping and handling for first guide, $5.00 for each additional guide	
Total	

Worldwide orders accepted with U.S. funds. Add $35.00 per business guide for shipping. To ensure delivery we mail air parcel post only. Prices subject to change without notice. Allow 3-4 weeks for delivery. **No C.O.D.s.**

SUBSCRIBE NOW!

To qualify for lower prices, see below for information on subscribing to *Entrepreneur Magazine*. If you are already a subscriber, write your subscription number from the label of a recent magazine here: _____

Yes! I want the subscriber discount that comes with my subscription to *Entrepreneur*. I understand I will receive a $10.00 discount on any Entrepreneur guide, **except guides priced at $29.50.** (In Canada add $10 per year. Overseas orders add $20 per year.)

Start my subscription at the basic rate checked:
- ❏ 3 years (save 57% off cover price) $47.97
- ❏ 2 years (save 50% off cover price) $37.97
- ❏ 1 year (save 46% off cover price) $19.97

Payment by:
❐ Check or money order enclosed

Charge my: ❏ VISA   ❐ MasterCard   ❐ Discover   ❐ Am Exp

Credit Card # _____ Expiration Date _____

Sign Here _____ (No orders shipped without exp. date & signature)

Name _____

Address _____

City _____ State _____ Zip _____

May we have your phone # in case we have questions regarding your order?

Work Phone ( ) _____ Home Phone ( ) _____

Mail to: 2392 Morse Avenue • P.O. Box 19787 • Irvine, CA 92713-9438   **9N184**
Call toll free: 1-(800) 421-2300 • in California 1-(800) 352-7449

CALL TOLL FREE 1-(800) 421-2300
in California 1-(800) 352-7449